John D. Rockefeller

Biography of the Richest and Most Ruthless Business Titan in History

By

Nathan Anderson

Please consult a licensed professional before attempting any techniques outlined in this book.

By reading this document, the reader agrees that under no circumstances is the author responsible for any losses, direct or indirect, that are incurred as a result of the use of information contained within this document, including, but not limited to, errors, omissions, or inaccuracies.

Table of Contents

Introduction

The Rockefeller name is a name that is incredibly rooted into a variety of disparate realms throughout the United States. Perhaps this is due to the fact that the family's legacy is so unlike any others in the way that they formulated their wealth on a level that was simply unprecedented during those times. Having such strongholds in the oil industry, banking on Wall Street, the arts, medical research, and higher education, the Rockefeller family has boasted indisputable influences on the realms that they have been involved in.

This biography, however, is purely focused on one member of the Rockefeller family. John D. Rockefeller Sr. found his way into the history books for not only being widely considered the richest American man and one of the wealthiest individuals in modern history but also one of the greatest American philanthropists and business magnates of all time. Rockefeller was someone who could not possibly have fathomed at an early age the wealth that he would one day accrue. Though he was undoubtedly someone who had dreamt of it during the earliest years of his life. This can be found as he once famously stated that he dreamt of one day having $1,000,000 and living to be 100 years of age. Though the latter would be a goal he did not make, the former was something that he had reached and surpassed by a long stretch.

John Davison Rockefeller was born in upstate Richford, New York, to a rather large family. The Rockefeller family would find themselves moving many times during the young Rockefeller's childhood before they would eventually find themselves settling down in Cleveland, Ohio. This is really where the story of John D. Rockefeller Sr. would begin. From becoming an assistant bookkeeper at only 16 years of age, the young Rockefeller would have had no idea where his life would eventually take him. His wealth would soar in the world of kerosene and gasoline, and the ultimate wealth that he would accrue during those times is overwhelming, even by our modern-day standards.

Throughout it all, however, he asserted that it was his religion and his family that truly set the stage for being the ultimate guiding force that would lead him throughout his life. In fact, he truly and devotedly believed that it was his faith that was the ultimate key to his overwhelmingly successful life. He also maintained a staunch capitalist approach and ideology in the theory of Social Darwinism. In fact, he was quoted more than once stating that, "The growth of a large business is merely a survival of the fittest." Rockefeller was a strikingly humble man, and he did not let a lot of personal things get to him. If he was dealt a blow, he allowed it to hit him and then simply turned the tables so that the cards were dealt in his favor. He was an astute and studious man who was able to truly see through the business world and make things work in his favor, regardless of the cost.

There is a tremendous amount of wealth (figuratively speaking, of course) that we can gather from John D. Rockefeller in the spectrum of both information and knowledge. In fact, it is simply incredible what we can learn from one of the most influential and successful men of the 19th and 20th centuries. Rockefeller was an intelligent man of both mystery and intrigue, and he was also a man who had set in motion a path to success and wealth and could not have had any idea that he was to become just as successful as he was. From the get-go, he was a man with a vision and a dream, and he would stop and nothing to reach his dreams of success. From the highs to the lows of his life, this is the biography of John D. Rockefeller Sr.

Chapter One:
The Early Years

Not a tremendous amount of information is known about the earliest days of the Rockefeller family's origins. The Rockefeller family were German immigrants who had first settled in Pennsylvania, then in New Jersey, where they would remain until the year 1832. John D. Rockefeller's grandparents, Godfrey and Lucy Rockefeller, would eventually move northwest, against the desires of Godfrey, who wanted to move to Michigan. The family would make their way to Richford, New York, where Godfrey had recently purchased land. The journey, however, would prove no simple feat and would, in fact, take roughly two years of travel by walking beside a covered wagon. Godfrey and Lucy would be accompanied by all of their children except for one; their 22-year-old son, William "Bill" Avery Rockefeller, who had a knack for leaving his family for extended periods of time. Though he would rejoin his family in Richford in 1835, roughly a year after they had already settled in.

The town of Richford, New York, was, and remains to this day, a small town with not a tremendous amount of history that lies upon it. The town itself was founded in 1808, and it was settled by the year of 1813, with the first tavern having been built in 1817. There really was not too much else that gave this town something to boast about. While there are rumors of the area having some pretty significant ties to the Underground Railroad, Richford really has nothing else more to offer other than a peaceful, quiet, and more relaxed way of living. In fact, according to the 2010 census, a mere 1,172 people reside there. But, there is something that the small town of Richford does, in fact, have to offer those who visit it.

In fact, Richford has something that brings people from across the globe to visit this quaint town. It lays claim to being the birthplace of the founder of the Standard Oil Company, and is also one of the wealthiest men in modern history. In fact, the foundation of John D. Rockefeller's childhood can still be found, marked by a sign that designates the site as one of historical value and lays alongside what is now called, "Rockefeller Road." A historical sign that sets the place as being the home to one of the most successful and influential men in all of history.

When Bill Rockefeller showed up in Richford, he arrived in a tavern with a piece of slate around his neck asking where the residence of Godfrey Rockefeller was. He was pretending to be a mute and deaf peddler. He found that using this method allowed him the opportunity to get more information from people in order to be able to use that information for his own benefit. It is more than likely that this was how he gained information about a wealthy landowner by the name of Davison, who owned property about 30 miles northwest of Richford. He had learned that Davison had a pretty young daughter, only 24 years of age, who had a nice price that would come along with her to whomever she decided to marry. As Bill was already quite prevalent in peddling, and as he was all too familiar with the area, he decided to head that direction to meet Davison, and his daughter, Eliza, himself.

Though he was still pretending to be deaf and mute when he arrived at the Davison's farm, he had proved to make quite an impression on Eliza. Bill boasted a full red beard, wore fancy embroidered waistcoats that were made out of silk, and the manner to which he simply appeared out of nowhere provided him with an almost whimsical and magical fantasy of sorts to Eliza. Even though she fell for "the peddler," she once stated that she would have married Bill anyway, deaf and mute or not. He captured her fancy and held it. He eventually would go on to play off his deaf and mute peddler act as nothing more than a joke, and he and Eliza began courting. The joke was not very funny, however, to Eliza's father, who forewarned her that she would be miserable if she married Bill. She was young and in love, however, and also old enough to marry who she desired whether her parents approved or not. The two would shortly thereafter be married at a friend's home, as her father would not allow the wedding to take place at his home. He also refused to attend the wedding.

Bill Rockefeller would build a small home for his new bride that was located less than a half a mile away from his own parents' homestead. There were no neighbors located in close proximity to Bill and Eliza's home, so throughout the first few years of marriage, Eliza would spend a good majority of her time at her in-laws home, particularly while Bill was away, and he more often than not would leave without even telling her. Eliza would often struggle finding her place in her new family. Her father-in-law was a raging alcoholic, her husband was a loud, boisterous man who was rarely around, and the other Rockefellers were simply above her energy levels. During family events, she often would retreat to another part of the small home to find some quiet solitude. Her mother-in-law would often join her. The two women found solace in one another, as both were incredibly intelligent, devoutly religious, soft-spoken, and had ultimately made the wrong choice in their life partner.

John Davison Rockefeller was born on July 8th, 1839, in Richford, to father William Avery Rockefeller Sr. and mother, Eliza Davison, and he had seven siblings: Clorinda, Cornelia, Francis, Frank, Lucy, Mary Ann, and William. There is surprisingly little information that can be found about his relationship with his siblings.

John's father, William Rockefeller, was a self-proclaimed, "traveling botanic salesman," which is basically just a fancy name for a snake oil salesman. In other words, he was a salesman who knowingly sold products that were basically placebos. These salesmen made such well-versed and believable claims that their elixirs could cure virtually anything that people all but threw their money at them to get their hands on the hottest new product that boasted claims of making you live longer, healing the lame, or simply looking better. Though he often posed as a deaf-mute peddler, his larger-than-life personality and cut-above-the-rest sales tactics earned him the nicknames "Big Bill" or "Devil Bill."

As a traveling salesman, William Rockefeller also was living a double life with another woman in another town by the name of Nancy Brown, to whom he also married and had children with using the name Dr. William Levingston while posing as an ear and eye specialist. Though he was great in his sales position selling magical elixirs, by the time he rolled back to Richford, there was never enough money to care for Eliza and his children with her, so finances were always a struggle for the Rockefeller family during the early years. Though that was not something that set the family back, the Rockefellers would always fight to live a comfortable life, not wealthy, but just having enough to get by.

William taught his children to never trust anyone. And there are stories of William telling a young John to jump into his arms so that he could catch him, but in turn, simply allowing him to fall to the floor. He was also notorious for using abundant claims and promises to con his children into doing extra chores and always going back on his promises. William is famously quoted as to saying that, "I cheat my boys every chance I get. I want to make 'em sharp." This strained relationship with his father was one that, while not necessarily admirable, was one that would forever shape the man who John Davison Rockefeller would inevitably become, and it was that relationship that drove him to the burning desire to find ultimate success in his own life.

John was the eldest of his siblings, and when his father was away he took on the role of man of the house, helping his mother to do odd jobs, including selling turkeys for meat to help make ends meet for the family. John was known in his family to be a proud and hardworking man. He would pick up slack in the house when it was needed in order to ensure that his family's home and family as a whole were taken care of and provided for to the very best of his ability as a young boy. He was undoubtedly a hard worker and quite a driven young man, even at the earliest of ages.

His mother, Eliza, was devoutly religious and an incredibly well-disciplined woman. She was also the very first person to have taught John to work hard, save his money, and to diligently and generously give back to charities and be generous with his money. When he was only 12 years of age, he had managed to save approximately $50 from simply doing odd side jobs for nearby neighbors while also helping his mother out with raising, caring for, and butchering the turkeys that the family owned. His mother would, in turn, urge him to loan that $50 that he had saved to a local farmer while also charging a seven percent interest fee that was to be paid back to him within a year. The farmer had successfully kept his end of the bargain and he paid John back (along with the applied interest) the following year. The young Rockefeller was so incredibly pleased with his financial return that he once stated, "The impression was gaining ground with me that it was a good thing to let the money be my servant and not make myself a slave to the money..."

The family would eventually move to Owego, New York, in 1851, and up until the year 1852, Rockefeller would attend the Owego Academy, where he highly excelled at math, particularly mental arithmetic in which his instructors would go on to note that he was more than capable of being able to problem-solve some of the most difficult arithmetic in his head. This sort of mental arithmetic was something that would go on to prove quite useful to him as his career would continue to grow. Rockefeller was noted to be an average student when it came to other subjects, however, it should also be noted that his parents always ensured that the quality of his education was exceptionally high. Rockefeller never really had a lot of friends while he was in school, but he also wasn't considered to be unpopular, either. He had a very dry sense of humor that rarely was exposed, but when it was it was met with surprising laughs from those around him. He rarely displayed his personal emotions and always appeared controlled and collected, which was undoubtedly a trait that he ensured he kept throughout his lifetime.

Eventually, Big Bill's double life would catch up to him, and he ended up confessing to both Eliza and Nancy of his extramarital affairs with each woman, and he then proposed to both of the women that they all move in together and simply formulate a bigamist relationship (which, while frowned upon, was certainly not illegal in the United States at the time). As smooth a talker as Big Bill was, he convinced both of the women to formulate one big relationship, with the women acting as "sister-wives" of a sort, for a time. When questions were pressed, they asserted that Nancy was the family housekeeper. When Eliza's father found out what was happening in the home of his daughter, he purchased a small home for Nancy and her children, and she was all but forbidden to have anything to do with the family ever again.

The family would all uproot and move their lives to Cleveland, OH, in the year 1853. A young John watched this all unfold and found himself to be disgusted by his father's actions and proclaimed that not only would he never follow in his footsteps, but he would also work hard, save his money, and never spend frivolously. At around the same time, he also became incredibly religious and deeply rooted in the church, and he regularly attended Sunday worship services. It was the actions of his father that really was the starting point for the early desire to begin working as soon as he could find work so that he could save up enough money to leave his family.

When the family moved to Cleveland, John would attend Cleveland Central High School where, again, he excelled in math, was pretty average in other subjects, and he also decided to take on joining the Debate Team (yet another skill that would highly benefit him in his future career endeavors). However, he had no desire to be forced to have to wait until he graduated to begin working and ultimately start his life and career endeavors. He ultimately would end up dropping out of school in the spring of 1855 and enrolled in a 10-week business and accounting class at Folsom Mercantile College, where he would learn banking and exchange, single and double-entry bookkeeping, mercantile customs, penmanship, and commercial history.

Unfortunately, it was around this time that Eliza and John found out that Bill was having yet another affair with a teenage girl named Margaret Allen, to whom he was legally married to in Canada. Bill was becoming increasingly more distant from Eliza and his children and thought it best to spend most of his time in Canada with his new family. While he was still in high school, John approached the principal of his school to request assistance in helping his family find a new, more suitable home. The principal, Dr. White, opened the doors to his own home to the family. For reasons unknown but not truly surprising, young John would proclaim that his mother was a widow to Dr. White. He was more than likely attempting to shield his mother from countless questions over the status of her husband and why he was so often gone, thus leading to further questions about the man's character. Eliza would find herself living as a "widow" for the duration of her marriage to Bill. Upon making his fortune, John purchased a ranch for his father and would regularly send him money at his request. He only made one request, which was to leave his Canadian wife and return to his mother and true family. Bill always refused the request, and when he passed away, he was buried in a small plot under his alias, "William Levingston." He also made sure that Margaret Allen or her children never received any access to the Rockefeller inheritance.

While for the most part, Rockefeller learned all of the things not to do as a man from his father, there were certain lessons that he gained from him. In fact, one of the most important things that Rockefeller had learned from his father was how to carefully and successfully draw up notes and other sorts of vitally important business-related documents. Rockefeller's father was an incredibly meticulous man when it came to business matters, and he was notably a firm believer in terms of the importance of both making and keeping business contracts.

Unfortunately, business in Cleveland during the mid-19th century was actually quite poor at the time that Rockefeller began his job search in the fall of 1855, and he had found himself faced with a number of issues in finding a decent job. It should also be noted that Cleveland was not as large a city during those years as it is to this day, and though he was always sharply dressed, typically wearing a black tie and dark suit, Rockefeller found that most of the businesses he had inquired at (many he would visit upwards of three times just to inquire as to a yes or a no to a job) simply could not afford to hire him. Rockefeller was such an incredibly driven young man that he took the job search as more than that; he took it as a complete learning experience. When he applied for a job and was turned down, he asked questions as to why he was being turned down and what he could do to improve himself. He then would go on to the next company on his list. By the time he finished visiting every company on his list, about a month would have passed, and he would circle back around to those businesses to see if they were ready to hire just yet.

Rockefeller was also adamant about not settling for just any sort of job. He easily could have found a job that tended to hire hardworking teenage boys, such as working in a shop as an assistant. He avoided small establishments that would prove to be nothing more than just another dead-end job. He once said of his early job searching days that, "I went to the railroads, the banks, the wholesale merchants. I did not go to any small establishments. I did not guess what the job would be, but I was after something big." Instead, he drove forward in finding the career that he knew he would be good at, excel at, learn from, and also set him up for having success in the long run as well.

While he had not gained a tremendous amount of knowledge at the mercantile college, it was a sustainable enough amount of information that allowed him the opportunity to finally get an assistant bookkeeping position at Hewett and Tuttle after nearly two whole months of searching. An interesting fact is that after he was interviewed successfully, it was his flawless penmanship that solidified him landing the position on September 25th, 1855 at the mere age of 16. Hewett and Tuttle was a local commission merchant and produce shipper. While he obtained a tremendous amount of knowledge, he went unpaid for the first three months of work, and then the job only paid him fifty cents per day, which is the modern equivalent of about$13.36. This is not even close to being a paycheck he could have comfortably lived on by himself, and that most certainly was his ultimate goal.

However, John always worked diligently, and he took his job quite seriously. He was exact, precise, and always incredibly honest. He would never make out a false bill of lading, and always would go to great measures to collect dues from those who had outstanding accounts. He was patient, persistent, and a notably pleasant young man to be around. John truly loved his job, and he loved and thrived on the work. He had been keeping the family books for his mother, so this job came as second nature to him, and he was not only incredibly good at his duties, but he made the work seem effortless and purely enjoyable.

Oftentimes in the business world, we come to see that those who truly enjoy their jobs actually do better in the position than those who have been doing the same work for an extensive amount of time. This was most certainly the case with John D. Rockefeller. He picked things up quickly and got the work done fast and without error. In fact, John was a better accountant than either of the senior accountants that worked at Hewett and Tuttle. Whether they noticed the fact or not, John most certainly did, and it gave him an utter sense of satisfaction. John was largely in charge of collections in the firm and would go over the bills with such closeness that he never made a mistake. While the vast majority of accountants would simply pass the bill to the customer and the customer would pay it, John took it to a more personal level and would go over the finances with the customer. If an error was made in their presence, whether it be larger or smaller than the bottom line figure, he would correct it in front of the customer in the most honest of ways.

Though he was a debt collector, often a thankless job, John still held himself with the utmost pride, patience, and politeness as he could muster. It has been said that John would often sit outside of the businesses of those who owed the firm money for hours on end until the business owners would eventually cave in and go outside to pay him. He didn't favor the debt collection as much as he did sitting quietly back at the office managing the figures and finances at his desk. He once stated that he often had very bad dreams during those years and even into his older years. When he was of quite old age, he admitted, "how many times I dreamed now and then up to recent years that I was trying to collect those bills. I would wake up exclaiming, 'I can't collect So-and-So's account!'"

Young John, even from the earliest of ages, had found himself fascinated with money. His father would come home from his travels when John was a very young boy and upon returning would always bring the family buckets filled with cash and coins. This was a magical thing to John, and he wanted a part of having his own fortune. Though as a Christian man he knew that it was a sin to be blinded by gold, he found a sort of balance by being cautious of greed but still pursuing a comfortable lifestyle that could set him free from his father's hold and still be able to help support his family.

John would become quite heavily involved in the Erie Street Mission Baptist Church in Cleveland, and it was here where he would find a true foundation in his faith in terms of reaching a higher, more intimate level. The church would become like a second family to him. When he was paid, though not much, he would always make sure to tithe his paycheck to the Erie Street Mission Baptist Church while also giving back to local area charities. Between work and his church morals, Rockefeller was left with very little free time to associate with others. He did not frequent taverns, did not associate with women of "loose morals," et cetera. The social events that he did attend were events that were put on by his church, and he would often frequent them to socialize. Though he would often admire the pretty ladies, he was never rude nor did he engage in immoral behavior. He was a quiet man who never let his emotions get the best of him. His emotional releases would always come at Sunday services in which he could worship, pray, and let the stresses of his everyday life pass from him.

He was utterly devoted to both work and his church, and after his large, very public successes would be made years later, one lady who was also a member of his congregation at the time commented that, "In those years... Rockefeller might have been found there any Sunday sweeping out the halls, building a fire, lighting the lamps, cleaning the walks, ushering people to their seats, studying the Bible, praying, singing, performing all the duties of an unselfish and thorough going church member... He was nothing but a clerk and had little money, and yet he gave something to every organization in the little, old church. He was always very precise about it. If he said that he would give fifteen cents, not a living soul could move him to give a penny more or a penny less... He studied his Bible regularly and diligently, and he knew what was in it." Not only did he tithe without waver, he also set aside a portion of his salary to simply give away to those in need that he met on the street. Interestingly, we can confirm all of this information because Rockefeller kept just as close and accurate track of his personal finances as he did those of the ones he handled at Hewett and Tuttle.

While the job never amounted to much for him in terms of financial wealth, Rockefeller was always incredibly proud of that first job. In fact, so much so that he celebrated September 26th every year until he died as his own personal holiday in which he deemed, "Job Day." He considered "Job Day" to be even more important than his own birthday and was once quoted later in his life as to saying, "All my future seemed to hinge on that day, and I often tremble when I ask myself the question: 'What if I had not got the job?'"

By 1858, he had more responsibilities at Hewitt and Tuttle than he initially had. Rockefeller would have to arrange quite complex transportation deals which generally would involve transporting single shipments of freight by either lake boats, canals, or the railroad. Rockefeller would also start to become involved in various trading ventures by his own accord as well. He was known to be a man who was cautious by nature, and he would only pursue business ventures if he could successfully calculate that the deal would be a successful one. Upon careful reviews of a direct course of action, Rockefeller would, in turn, act both boldly and quite quickly to see the venture through to its fruition. Rockefeller had nerves of steel, and he was highly regarded for being able to process through quite complex deals free and clear of any sense of hesitation.

Rockefeller would inevitably end up making the decision to leave Hewett and Tuttle after he had gotten into a disagreement with one of the partners of the firm regarding the amount of a raise that he was promised. He harbored no ill will against the firm upon leaving it. He had never actually intended to permanently stay there. And when he felt that his services were not valued in terms of how much he was actually making, he opted to make the ultimate decision to venture out on his own.

It was this unique combination of resolve, precision, and a sense of caution that would soon bring him some attention and a greater sense of respect in terms of Cleveland's business community. Rockefeller was quite popular in his community, and over a period of just a few years, he had gained both trust and notoriety amongst community members. Because of this, he was able to start his own business with a man by the name of Maurice Clark in 1857. Maurice was a former classmate of John's, and the two men had each obtained $2,000 (approximately $100,000 today), which granted the men the opportunity to begin investing and trading in goods such as grain, meat, and hay. And, in their first year of business, they had found themselves grossing more than $450,000. While they had to pay back initial loans and pay off several things, this was still a substantial amount of money to have been earned by the young Rockefeller and was the very start of what would prove to be an incredibly long, affluent career. Business was incredibly competitive in Cleveland at the time. And the success that Clark & Rockefeller had found was largely due to the natural business capabilities that Rockefeller boasted.

By the year 1859, Clark and Rockefeller had expanded so largely that they would take on another partner. George Gardner, the former mayor of Cleveland, would team up with the men, and Rockefeller's name would ultimately end up being dropped from the firm's company sign largely due to the fact that Gardner brought with him a substantial amount of capital for the firm. This left Rockefeller with a bit of a sour taste in his mouth after having lost his status as an equal partner within the firm, however, it would be the fact that his partners, more often than not, would shun the austerity of Rockefeller's character that truly got to him. Rockefeller was a man who never opted to make exuberant purchases, and yet his partners did so in abundance, which truly upset Rockefeller. Gardner and Clark ultimately purchased a yacht, much to the dismay of Rockefeller. He even outright refused to see the boat when offered. Rockefeller expressed his disdain towards the purchase, stating, "George Gardner, you're the most extravagant young man I even knew! The idea of a young man like you, just getting a start in life, owning interest on a yacht! You're injuring your credit at the banks - your credit and mine! No, I won't go on your yacht. I don't even want to see it." To which, Gardner would reply, "John, I see that there are certain things which you and I probably will never agree. I think you like money better than anything else in the whole world, and I do not. I like to have a little fun along with business as I go through life."

John most certainly was not wrong in his belief system, particularly with regards to banking and the credit of the firm. John was the one who had success with regards to borrowing on behalf of the firm. The financial community of Cleveland respected Rockefeller's grounded ideologies in terms of his financial habits and his lack of vices. He was an upstanding member of the community and his church, and it was his success as a borrower that ultimately would be the key to his success. He was able to successfully obtain large loans to build his capital to do any business he needed simply because he was such an upstanding member of the community. This is not something that Gardner and Clark could have achieved of their own accord.

Chapter Two:

The Oil Boom

In the mid-1850's, crude oil that did not come directly from the ground was viewed as nothing more than a nuisance and a pollutant that made water undrinkable. Though many Native American tribes used the oil that skimmed their water sources in full abundance for medicinal purposes, skin liniments, and paint, oil truly meant nothing to anyone. That is, until August 27, 1859, when a man named Edwin Drake would strike oil near the town of Titusville in Pennsylvania. This would, in turn, spark a frenetic oil boom in a region that would soon become regarded as the "oil region" of the northwest territory of Pennsylvania. Edwin Drake was also an employee to a group of investors of the Pennsylvania Rock Oil Company that was based in New Haven, Connecticut. The investors had attained a sample of oil from Pennsylvania and had a chemist from Yale University test it. The chemist found that the Pennsylvanian oil was some of the highest quality he had seen and informed the investors that the oil could easily be refined for use in a wide array of different products.

During the mid-19th century, a typical well could be drilled for water or, more interestingly, brine (which could be refined in order to obtain salt). It was through the process of salt drilling where many would note that they would get an oil seepage into their salt wells, and this would spark the idea of a drilling for oil concept. The method of testing oil, refining oil, and the technology that Drake had utilized for initially obtaining the oil were not things that were new at that time, in fact, the oil industry was actually pretty advanced in 1859. However, a new sort of technology was in the works that would promote ease and speed in the ability to obtain oil: pumping it out of the ground like water. And that, once perfected, would change everything.

In 1860, the Civil War broke out, and Rockefeller, only 21 years of age at the time, was a self-proclaimed abolitionist and an avid supporter of the Union forces. Rockefeller's younger brother, Frank, was desperate to join the Union army and begged his older brother to loan him the $75 needed to become outfitted as a Union soldier. John would ultimately loan him the money, and Frank would end up becoming wounded early in the war at Cedar Mountain and Chancellor. These events that unfolded between the two would lead to a permanent tumultuous relationship between the two brothers, as Frank felt that he had paid a severe price, while his successful older brother had the opportunity to avoid it and was met with wealth beyond either of their wildest imaginations.

John himself was drafted. He received an exemption due to the fact that he was considered the primary means to support his family. This was largely due to the fact that three years prior, when John was only 18 years of age, his father sent him enough money to build a home for Eliza and John's four children. This was ultimately his way of cutting ties with his former family and would make John the breadwinner and caretaker for his mother and siblings. Not only could he not have gone to war for this reason alone, but it also put his business at risk as a whole. Rockefeller, in turn, set about paying a professional soldier to go in his place so that he could still contribute to the war while continuing to be able to successfully run his business. The fee to pay for a replacement soldier was$300, and Rockefeller made this payment by outfitting a Union company of 30 men placed under the command of Captain Levi Scofield, who was a close personal friend of Rockefeller, in addition to paying the $300 fee. He was once quoted as saying, "I wanted to go in the army and do my part, but it was simply out of the question. There was no one to take my place. We were a new business and if I had not stayed it must have stopped-- and with so many dependent on it." Hiring professional soldiers was actually quite common practice for those who could have afforded to do so during the Civil War, and it also allowed the opportunity for profits to be made for those who stayed behind in the way of selling supplies for the war effort.

The latter part of the 1850s would truly bring about a boom for oil as a cheap and reliable way of lighting one's home. In 1862, Rockefeller would begin tossing the idea around of getting involved in the oil industry himself. During the Civil War, Clark and Rockefeller's business would grow and expand quite rapidly. As previously stated, as the prices of items such as grain went up, so did the men's commissions. The vast majority of Clark and Rockefeller's selling would be done based solely on commission, and that led to Clark and Rockefeller taking zero risks in terms of fluctuations in pricing. Rockefeller was an incredibly planned, calculated, and extremely precise individual, and in no way did he prefer to take a gamble. He was a man who tended to avoid financial risks and would adamantly refuse loans and advances in smaller amounts on a localized level (such as in the way of a friend or family member), and he tended to turn, instead to large banks to borrow increased amounts of money that would go about assisting him in handling shipments for his business. It was this more aggressive style that would go on to build up the men's business every single year.

The first decade of the oil boom (the 1860s) proved to be quite a difficult feat for men who pumped oil from the ground. The process in its entirety was incredibly time-consuming, difficult, and strenuous. The small towns that surrounded the oil regions of Pennsylvania were incredibly rural, and many of them were not even accessible by railroad, nor did the vast majority of them have access to telegraph offices. Men who drilled for oil found themselves in the position of getting it out of the ground, storing it in barrels that leaked, and then simply having to wait for a representative from one of the nearby oil refineries to come and pick up the oil in order to be able to sell the product. Most of these representatives would arrive via horseback to collect as a good majority of the roads were simply not passable by way of wagon. This was incredibly strenuous in the way of finances as well for the oil drillers as they had to take a hefty price cut on their oil largely due to how much it cost the oil refiners to come and pick up the crude oil in the first place. To put it simply, oil rigging in the earliest days was often nothing more than a lose-lose situation for those who were actually going about gathering the crude oil in the first place.

Though Rockefeller was intrigued by this new oil boom, he remained ever-cautious with regards to diving into such a new, uncertain endeavor. Initially, Rockefeller would only trade oil as simply another sort of commodity along the side of the typical foodstuffs that were sold by the company. Rockefeller took it upon himself to visit the oil regions of Pennsylvania in 1861. It took this to really convince Rockefeller that the oil industry was the field that he desperately wanted to become involved in. When he saw the infrastructures that sprang up around the oil wells, he felt a sort of "gold rush" as he would once say, and this really sealed the deal for his desire to jump on board. The oil boomtowns that could be found throughout the regions of the oil wells were fueled with all of the things that the tight-belted, devout Baptist man utterly loathed and would leave him horrified. The mud-caked streets were lined with makeshift taverns that were filled with prostitutes, drinking, and gambling, and Rockefeller desperately wanted to take control of the reins in order to bring the oil industry under a more refined and organized manner of business.

In 1863, Clark and Rockefeller would eventually expand and take on a new partner, an Englishman by the name of Samuel Andrews, who had previously worked in a Cleveland-based lard-oil refinery. Andrews brought with him the knowledge that he had discovered: that by way of refining crude oil, it could, in turn, be converted into kerosene. Which, at the time, was a well-protected formula. Unfortunately, however, he simply lacked the knowledge that was required for both business and transportation of goods, and he did not have the funds to open up his own oil refinery.

The largest break for Andrews would come in the way that he was a member of the very same church that Rockefeller attended, therefore, Clark and Rockefeller were the first firm that Samuel Andrews would reach out and make his pitch to. Andrews was requesting a start-up fee of $8,000, and when his idea was pitched to Maurice Clark, it was met with heavy disdain. Clark asserted that the firm could only offer Andrews a mere$250, and with that, Andrews rushed into Rockefeller's office and found that John was significantly more intrigued by what Andrews had to say, thus offering him a $4,000 offer for the start-up of his refinery. Though this seemed like a hefty investment, even to Rockefeller, none of the men at the firm could have possibly fathomed just what a lucrative investment it would prove to be in the long run.

Before the start of the Civil War, the vast majority of people illuminated their homes by way of lamps that were fueled by a product called camphene. Camphene was a derivative of turpentine; however, the largest suppliers were predominantly located in southern regions of the United States, which had utterly been decimated by Union forces during the Civil War. Furthermore, the Civil War had also significantly interrupted the whaling business, which led to a heavily increased demand for kerosene. Prior to the war, the nation's most predominant demand was by and large cotton, however, following the war, the demand for kerosene was much greater. Oil refining into kerosene also led to a number of byproducts being created. Some of these byproducts included, but were certainly not limited to, petroleum jelly, paraffin, and benzene. Rockefeller's Standard Works (the name that was given to the company upon the second refinery being purchased by Rockefeller and Andrews) was ready to make all of these products readily available to their consumers for purchase.

Interestingly, the only byproduct that no one seemed to have any use for was that of gasoline. This was largely due to the fact that since automobiles had yet to be invented, gasoline was simply a useless commodity. Unfortunately, as there was not a need for gasoline, it was simply poured into the ground to get rid of it, and it ultimately would seep into the ground and pollute water. Of course, this act was done before people knew anything about pollution and the effects that such an act had on the environment. In addition to wreaking havoc on the environment, this act of discarding gasoline also got to the point of becoming incredibly dangerous. Captains of steamboats were no longer able to shovel coal overboard their vessels because they ran the risk of setting the water on which the steamboats ran completely on fire. By the year 1869, kerosene supplies were so ample that they exceeded demand. However, wells and oil refineries could quickly be decimated by a fire. Countless people lost not only their financial investments but on several occasions their lives to these fires as well. This was a huge risk, and it often kept Rockefeller up at night with stress. He knew he ran the risk of losing everything he had invested in should a fire ever break out at any one of his personal oil refineries, in addition to the stresses that he felt of the unknown, which included the oil fields ever drying up. Whenever Rockefeller found himself overwhelmed with these stresses and he felt himself questioning if he should back out of the oil industry, he would turn to his faith and trust the fact that God had blessed men with oil and that it would be a sustainable enough product to illuminate the nation and bless his business throughout the years.

More than likely anticipating Rockefeller and his partners to eventually make their move to enter into the oil industry at some point, the Atlantic and Great Western Railroad would expand into Cleveland later that year. The Atlantic and Great Western Railroad line traveled east into Meadville, Pennsylvania, then it continued northeast into Corry,

Pennsylvania, and it then extended over the border and into the state of New York, where it finally united with the Erie Railroad. More importantly, the Atlantic and Great Western Railroad line had branches that headed straight for the heartland of the oil industry -- Franklin and Titusville, which opened up two routes from Cleveland to New York City, which were referred to as the New York Central to Lake Shore system and also the Atlantic and Great Western Railroad line to Erie connection. These railroad systems instantly provided Cleveland with a huge advantage over Pittsburgh in terms of transportation, due largely to the fact that the region was dominated by the Pennsylvania Railroad at the time.

Soon enough, Rockefeller, Clark, and Andrews were not simply refining their own oil, but they were also implementing measures to increase production and substantially lower costs. Rockefeller detested waste and dedicated a considerable amount of time and energy to increasing the overall efficiency and productivity of his oil refining business. Rockefeller was a firm believer in the fact that the main secret to having a successful career was attention; simply the attention to detail and ironing out all of the details before submitting to anything. It was due to this that he, instead of outsourcing a third party, bought land filled with white oak to make his own barrels for oil and bought his own horses and wagons to transport wood for his items, the aforementioned barrels, to be built in Cleveland, just to name a few things. Instead of simply outsourcing those jobs to a third party, he saved a hefty amount of money, thus putting more money into his pocket and into his business in the long run.

Maurice Clark would comment on just how much loving care and attention Rockefeller put forth into his refinery business in a manner that Clark had not seen before in Rockefeller, save for the time he spent at Erie Street Mission Baptist Church. He would go on to state, "John had abiding faith in two things - the Baptist creed and oil. Yet another one of Rockefeller's associates also agreed saying, "The only time I ever saw John Rockefeller enthusiastic was when a report came in from the creek that his buyer had secured a cargo of oil at a figure much below the market price. He bounded up from his chair with a shout of joy, danced up and down, hugged me, threw up his hat, acted like a madman so much so that I have never forgotten it." This is just one good and rare example of an overjoyed outburst by Rockefeller.

By 1865, the five partners, Rockefeller, Clark, Andrews, and two of Clark's brothers, had found themselves at a means to an end for their firm. They were simply unable to agree on the management and direction of the company, felt that Rockefeller was too prudish with regards to his decision-making abilities, and Rockefeller wanted to expand the business using his own vision and direction that he saw would lead to the ultimate success of the firm overall. So the men opted to decide it would be best to simply sell the business to one of them solely, at the highest bid.

On auction day, Clark appeared with his lawyer and Rockefeller, unsurprisingly, on his own. The bids would escalate in increments of $5,000 until it would be Clark who capitulated. Rockefeller would go on to comment on the auction, "Finally, it advanced to $60,000 and by slow stages to $70,000, and I almost feared for my ability to buy my business and have the money to pay for it. At last, the other side bid$72,000. Without hesitation, I said, 'Seventy-two thousand and five hundred." Mr. Clark then said: 'I'll go no higher, John; the business is yours.' Shall I give you a check for it now?' I suggested. 'No,' Mr. Clark said, "I'm glad to trust you for it; settle at your convenience."

And with the highest bid being made by Rockefeller in the amount of $72,500, he, along with Andrews as his partner, would go on to form what would be called Rockefeller & Andrews. Rockefeller quickly learned the ins and outs of the oil industry, and the company would merge with a very large oil refinery owner in Cleveland, OH. Rockefeller's company was growing quickly, and he ended up bringing his brother, William, and Andrew's brother, John, onto the team as well.

In 1869, the oil industry saw a bit of a decline, as there were more oil refineries that had been built than there was crude oil to be refined into kerosene. Roughly 90% of the oil refineries were falling short financially. During these incredibly trying times, a local Cleveland man by the name of John H. Alexander who owned a competing oil refinery made a proposal to Rockefeller that he would sell him his oil refinery business at merely a tenth of what it was valued at. The decline had greatly affected operations for Rockefeller's business as well, and it appeared to him for a brief moment that he stood to lose all that he had worked so hard for over the course of the last few years. However, he stood true to his unabating and unwavering devotion to God that he would be carried through the hard times and trusted the idea that oil was a gift from God to all of mankind. So, instead of crumbling with dismay, he opted to take risks and felt compelled that cooperation and not competition would be the key to his successes. However, many people felt that Rockefeller's tactics were more along the lines of the exact opposite and that Rockefeller was simply out to dominate and crush all of the competition by whatever means possible.

As previously stated, the main issue that the oil industry was dealing with was that there were too many oil refineries and not enough crude oil being delivered to them to be refined. The owners and operators of the oil refineries were not motivated by the risk of losing everything as the price of kerosene took a nosedive. Oil men were, instead, fueled with dreams of obtaining splendid wealth and bountiful fortunes overnight, thus leading them to simply keep on drilling and keep on building more oil refineries even though they were not making any money. In other words, there was more competition than the market was capable of being able to successfully support, and that led to all industry-related operations being impaired. Rockefeller came up with a solution, "a giant cartel that would reduce overcapacity, stabilize prices, and rationalize the industry." During the Civil War, a similar ideology was implemented by the oil refineries in Oil Creek, who were to become known as the Petroleum Producers' Association.

Rockefeller decided it would be in the best interest of his company to take advantage of the opportunity to buy all of the smaller oil refineries that were struggling the most. He did this with the idea in mind that doing so would cap production to levels that the market could handle. However, in order to successfully be able to accomplish this, he would need a tremendous amount of capital (more than ever before). Rockefeller's partner, Henry Flagler, would come up with the idea of the firm incorporating and selling shares to their investors. Therefore, Rockefeller, Andrews, and Flagler would be dissolved, and by January 10, 1870, the Standard Oil Company of Ohio was officially created. The ownership would consist of John D. Rockefeller holding 30% (he was also named president of the company), William Rockefeller holding 13.34%, Henry Flagler holding 16.67%, Samuel Andrews holding 16.67%, Stephen Harkness holding 13.34%, and Rockefeller's brother-in-law, O. B. Jennings, holding 10%. Together, Standard Oil Company would hold roughly 10% of the oil industry during the time of its actual formation. With the assistance of Flagler, Rockefeller purchased all of the smaller area oil refineries in and around Cleveland, leaving no competition to their new company. If a refinery opted to not sell to Rockefeller, he would drastically lower his prices so that the consumers flocked to him as opposed to his competitor, which would inevitably put that refinery completely out of business. In fact, it has also been said that one of the ways that Rockefeller would convince his competitors to sell their oil refineries to him was to simply invite them over and set down a book of his personal finances and then leave the room. The book granted the competitor the opportunity to see what Rockefeller could operate at as a loss, which was significantly longer than they could. This would leave them with the option to either sell their business to him or simply go bankrupt.

As Rockefeller's business within the confines of the oil industry grew, so did his needs for more capital in order to promote and ensure continued growth. From the get-go, Standard Oil was the biggest joint-stock corporation in the world, boasting a capital of over a million dollars. The banks of Cleveland were simply too small to be able to provide him with such required capital. Rockefeller had no other option but to turn to Wall Street in order to be able to successfully obtain the funds he needed to continue to grow. Wall Street bankers, however, were not too quick at investing in the oil industry at the time due largely to the threat of risk of total loss due to dry wells and fires. As John's younger brother, William, was more of the people person between the two, John felt that it would be in the best interest of the firm for him to head to New York to wheel and deal with the Wall Street bankers in order to sweet talk them into providing the firm with more capital. The backing of John's honesty and meticulous care for the organization of his business really spoke volumes to the Wall Street bankers. John was excellent at winning the trust of those around him but never gave off that he was too eager or in dire need of the funding. Even bankers who were quite skeptical of the oil industry itself were by no means skeptical of John D. Rockefeller.

In the eyes of Rockefeller, the oil business was nothing short of chaotic at the time. This was due largely to the fact that the entry costs in both oil drilling and refining were so low that the market was congested with crude oil along with an equally immense amount of waste. To Rockefeller, the idea of free competition simply could not work very well as there was too much of a mixture of very large, more highly efficient firms and equally as many small and medium firms that were less efficient. He felt that these smaller, weaker firms, as they attempted to challenge larger competition, did nothing more than drive down the cost of production, and, in turn, hurt the larger and more successfully run organizations. That was precisely why in 1871, Rockefeller began the process of formulating a plan to consolidate all oil refining firms into a single, well-managed organization in order to eliminate all of the excess price-cuts and capacity.

Chapter Three:
Rockefeller Takes Over

Although there are no written records to prove it, one thing that does prove this claim to be factual is that when the plan was initially formulated (in 1871) all of the largest banks in Cleveland joined with the Standard Oil Company, and they would also back Rockefeller and Flagler tooth and nail with regards to their incredibly vast expansion. Additionally, both Flagler and Rockefeller would come forward to confirm (more than 30 years later) that this plan was precisely what they set in motion.

Rockefeller and Flagler's carefully laid out plans would end up being interrupted by the 1871 South Improvement Scheme. The South Improvement Scheme was an idea that was implemented by a man named Tom Scott, who worked for the Pennsylvania Railroad. The idea was roused by way of the formulation of the 1868-1817 Anthracite Railroad combination whereby two coal companies and five railroads purchased all of the coal pits that laid alongside the five railroad systems in order to control both prices and output.

The South Improvement Company was developed in 1870 by the Pennsylvania Legislature, and its charter permitted it to be able to hold stocks from other companies that were located outside of the state. During this period of time, it was quite unusual to be able to assert this sort of power, and that made it perfect for the scheme of Tom Scott. He ended up arranging for the purchase of a charter from a group of Pittsburgh and Philadelphia oil refiners and Scott simply playing a quiet role in the backdrop. The scheme basically was nothing more than a proposal that was aimed to merge the railroads that carried oil in a pool. In other words, to simply unify oil refiners within one single organization: the South Improvement Company, while also binding together the two different elements in the way of agreements that would put an end to the damaging price-cuts and, in turn, restoring railroad freight charges to a significantly more profitable level.

In order to carry out the partnership of the refiners, a series of rebates was set in motion for refiners who conceded in signing on. This on its own would undoubtedly have coerced all of the oil refiners to combine, however, the clever plot failed to end with just that. In what would end up turning out to be a public relations catastrophe, those who were involved resolved to incorporate a drawback on all of the barrels that were to be shipped by all non-participants that would be equal to the standard rebate. Essentially, this was simply a tax on those who were non-participants with all of the profits being transferred to the oil refiners who were participants. Ironically, what planners failed to keep in mind was to keep producers in the loop of the scheme of things and despite attempts to assure drillers from the area's oil regions that the ultimate game plan would benefit them as well by ensuring that prices stayed up. This would ultimately lead to the Oil Regions Men revolting and, in turn, organizing a highly effective boycott against all of the railroads and oil refiners that they suspected were a part of the ultimate scheme. Ergo, the scheme ultimately would collapse in 1872 before it could even be carried out.

Many would go on to assume that Rockefeller himself was one of the original masterminds behind the South Improvement Company Scheme. The fact remains that he had not been a part of this particular scheme in terms of being a co-conspirator, however, both he and Flagler did in fact agree to engage and also participated in working quite hard to assist in setting the scheme up. Interestingly, one of the biggest issues that Rockefeller failed to do in his career was usher in his own side of the story with regards to his involvement with the scheme. This is due largely to the fact that it was his involvement in the scheme that made people question his morality in the first place, and it would go on to permanently contaminate his reputation. He would eventually go on to address the situation and stated, "Our silence encouraged the wildest romancers to spread wild tales about us." He also stated at a different time, "I shall never cease to regret that at that time we never called in the reporters."

In December 1871, as the South Improvement Company Scheme was attempting to cover up its tracks of wrongdoings Rockefeller and Flagler would move forward with their arrangement to centralize the industry. The two men went forward with their plan by first purchasing all of their competitors in the Cleveland area. Rockefeller handled all of the strategy, tactics, and negotiations with all of their competition firsthand, and he started out with the tenacious oil refineries first. He did so with the belief that if he purchased the weaker refineries before the stronger ones, he would then have to figure out how to handle higher prices at a later time and would also face more adversity and be met with more resistance by the stronger companies.

Rockefeller always sought to use the same technique. The company's merger would have to be affected with an increased capitalization of the Standard Oil and, in turn, the competing refinery would end up being appraised, the owners would be provided with a share of Standard Oil Company's stock based upon the company's value, and they would also be made partner in the Standard Oil Company. More proficient owners were also offered management positions at Standard Oil, and if they asked for cash up-front, they were given it. Though at later periods of time, there were a few owners who came forward to the press to say that they were treated unfairly, there is an overwhelming amount of evidence that would go on to prove that Standard Oil Company's rivals were paid more than fair prices for their company, even quite generous prices, and if they opted to accept Rockefeller's offer for stock shares in Standard Oil Company, they ended up becoming incredibly rich individuals.

Though his company was skyrocketing in terms of its success, the name Rockefeller was not yet a household name during those years. However, the South Improvement Company Scheme would go about changing all of that for Rockefeller. And not in the way that he would have preferred. It is not really quite clear just how the South Improvement Company planned on revealing the increased shipping rates. This is even more interesting to ponder due to the fact that Rockefeller's plans really didn't even work out in the way that he had planned with regards to the huge public outcry that took place once the plans of the scheme had come to light. Whether or not one is an admirer of Rockefeller, one thing can be made clear, and that is the fact that the South Improvement Company Scheme is truly nothing more than a secretive conspiracy that was aimed to utterly decimate smaller, independent oil refineries. With that in mind, it really does not matter how Rockefeller planned on announcing these rate increases, because once the word was leaked by accident, people were furious and his plans were rendered useless.

Word spread rampantly of the rate hikes, and the end result would lead to an uprising as Standard Oil Company swept up one refinery after another in the Cleveland area. By the time the South Improvement Company Scheme was dissipated, Standard Oil had control over 22 out of the 26 oil refineries in the area, and the scheme would be deemed "the Cleveland Massacre." One historian would go on to describe the result of the scheme, "For the horror-struck refiners in Titusville or Oil

City, this wasn't simply a new competitive threat: it was a death warrant, and they stopped work and poured into the streets, denouncing the action in strident tones." Hundreds of people would go on to flood opera houses and town halls to listen to speakers blatantly denouncing Rockefeller (who they deemed "the monster") and his co-conspirators (deemed the "40 thieves").

Throughout all of this, Rockefeller continued to remain calm, collected, and as composed as always. Never once did he waver, and he always remained true to his actions with regards to the takeover. To Rockefeller, there was absolutely nothing that was unethical in terms of securing rebates from railroad companies, and he most certainly was quite correct with the fact that if the Oil Creek refineries had the opportunity to get them, they would have done the exact same thing that he did. Rockefeller was a man who undoubtedly was strongly rooted in the Christian faith, which, one would think, would have led Rockefeller to question the tactics that he was implementing as he was certainly hearing all of the things that people were saying about him.

However, something that Rockefeller had learned to accomplish early on in his career was to refuse to listen to things that he would consider to be nothing more than gossip or idle chatter. Impassivity was a sort of defense mechanism that Rockefeller had to learn at quite a young age, due largely to the fact that his father's abysmal behavior led to plenty of gossip as he was growing up. Add in to the mix the fact that Cettie and John opted to confine their children to the constricts of their home; the Rockefellers firmly believed that if they were not loathed by the worldly society around them, they were not living their lives by their Christian fundamental beliefs. Rockefeller believed this so wholeheartedly that he once told a reporter, "I believe the power to make money is a gift from God - just as are the instincts for art, music, literature, the doctor's talent, the nurses, yours - to be developed and used to the best of our ability for the good of mankind. Having been endowed with the gift I possess, I believe it is my duty to make money and to use the money I make for the good of my fellow man according to the dictates of my conscience."

Years later, many of the individuals who had been bought out by the Standard Oil Company would go on to criminalize the men, particularly Rockefeller, who had been involved in the scheme. These individuals would go on to proclaim that they had been threatened into selling their businesses to the Standard Oil Company. However, Rockefeller adamantly refuted such statements, stating that he had never once threatened any owner of any of the companies and yet merely offered his own personal advice and insight which led to propositions being discussed and implemented towards a sale. It is interesting to note the fact that the "advice" Rockefeller often gave to the oil refinery owners was the fact that if they failed to sell their refinery to the Standard Oil Company, their company stood to lose it all within a year and that it would be in their best interest to just give it up and sell for some sort of a profit. To Rockefeller, he was doing nothing more than simply stating the obvious; that independent and small refineries simply could not withstand the state of the industry at that point in time. To the contrary, however, the owners of those small companies firmly believed that it was Rockefeller who was to blame for creating such an unstable environment where they felt they could have at least tried to survive, grow, and thrive.

Rockefeller was a man who was far from lacking emotions. He actually very genuinely cared for those around him. Which is one of the main reasons why, when the Standard Oil Company bought out a company, Rockefeller offered positions to those from the former company so that they would not have to be out of a job during those very trying times. It should also be noted that a good majority of the refineries that were purchased by the Standard Oil Company were purchased at higher rates than they were actually worth due to the fact that Rockefeller did not want to destroy anyone's livelihood. He was, in fact, attempting to do nothing more than control the rates at which oil was to be sold to the consumer. Some of the independent oil refineries he made arrangements with allowed the owners the opportunity to stay independently owned, providing the owners agreed to cap production at levels that were agreed upon by both parties. For a select few, however, Rockefeller opted to purchase their oil refinery at a very low price, matching the approximate price that the firms would have gone for at auction. Philanthropy was something that was of the utmost importance to Rockefeller; however, business was still business, and sometimes that meant eliminating things that stood in the way of building strong business for the good of the industry as a whole.

By the spring of 1872, Rockefeller had either merged with and/or purchased virtually all of the oil refineries in the Cleveland area. The refineries that were poorly constructed or simply not efficient enough by Rockefeller's standards were completely dismantled. The companies that were of higher quality were enhanced to meet the standards of Rockefeller and Flagler. Upon taking over Cleveland, Standard Oil Company had grown to an unprecedented size. All of the transactions that had taken place were kept in secret, and leaders of the Standard Oil Company were incredibly successful in keeping these secrets that a large number of their rival, independently owned oil refineries were left completely in the dark with regards to what was happening around them at the time.

The charter of the South Improvement Company would soon be revoked in Pennsylvania by the state legislature. This was largely due to public outcry against the firm and not because the firm had gone about violating any law or certain regulation. A month later, the South Improvement Company was superseded by an organization called the National Refiners' Association, or as it was more popularly referred, the Pittsburgh Plan. Whereby, the South Improvement Company was a secretive series of plans that were set in motion by the Standard Oil Company and three of the major railroads of the United States, the National Refiners' Association was extremely large and also incorporated public input into their decision-making process. It united the Standard Oil Company with three of the largest oil refiners in the Pittsburgh region: O.T. Waring, William Frew, and William G. Warden. While all of the oil refineries in Pittsburgh were invited to join the National Refiners' Association, the Oil Region's refiners loathed Rockefeller so vehemently that they blatantly refused to trust his true intentions, and they all simply believed that this was nothing more than a ploy to implement the very same actions that were undertaken by the South Improvement Company, just under a different name.

Oil refiner after oil refiner would come to Titusville, PA, to meet and discuss the terms for joining the National Refiners' Association. Rockefeller himself attended the vast majority of these meetings, and one of the refiners who attended one of the meetings went on to assert his opinion of what occurred during such negotiations. He stated, "One day several of us met at the office of one of the refiners, who, I felt pretty sure, was being persuaded to go into the scheme which they were talking up. Everybody talked except Mr. Rockefeller. He sat in a rocking chair, softly swinging back and forth, his hands over his face. I got pretty excited when I saw how those South Improvement men were pulling the wool over our men's eyes and making them believe we were all going to the dogs if there wasn't an immediate combination to put up the price of refined and prevent new people coming into the business, and I made a speech which, I guess, was pretty warlike. Well, right in the middle of it, John Rockefeller stopped rocking and took down his hands and looked at me. You never saw such eyes. He took me all in, saw just how much fight he could expect from me, and I knew it, and then up went his hands and back and forth went his chair."

The National Refiners' Association would last fewer than two months. The demise of it had less to do with the public outcry and more to do with the varying tactics that were being employed by the Oil Regions refiners. The sole purpose of the National Refiners' Association was the same of the South Improvement Company and that was to raise the prices of oil by simply reducing the amount of oil that was being refined at the time. However, many of the oil refineries that joined the National Refiners' Association quickly went back on those production caps just as soon as the prices of oil shot back up again. Many of the oil refinery owners also opted to sell their refineries to Rockefeller and then, in turn, took that money to buy another oil refinery with new and improved equipment. It was this sheer lack of cooperation and the games that the Pittsburgh refiners were playing with Rockefeller that led him to dub them "cheaters" and thus dissolve the National Refiners' Association as a whole.

However, the dissolution of the National Refiners' Association would not stop Rockefeller. He would make yet another attempt to gain the cooperation of the refineries: the "Treaty of Titusville." In the treaty, Rockefeller sought to convince refineries to pay double the rates that crude oil was going for at the time, and in turn, oil well owners could cap production rates at a level that everyone would agree to. Unfortunately, the Treaty of Titusville was met with the exact same issues as that of the National Refiners' Association; individual refineries were still opting to simply break their agreements at will. Rockefeller was finally faced with the fact that he simply could not control the individual refineries by simply placing them underneath a confederation of sorts. In order for him to get them to follow a set of standards, he needed to not only control the refineries but also the producers as well.

Throughout 1872, the Pennsylvania Railroad itself was seeking out various techniques to, like Rockefeller, utterly eliminate all of their competition and thus started charging extravagant rates for their services in the means of transporting oil to the oil refineries that were based in Pittsburgh. The ultimate plan of the Pennsylvania Railroad was to basically wipe Cleveland off the map in terms of being the center of the oil refining industry. This, in turn, led Cleveland oil refiners to start panicking and begin to think of different ways that they could start to transfer their bases of operation to Pennsylvania's Oil

Regions. This, of course, left the railroads of New York Central and Erie frantically scouring to recover their lost business.

As always, Rockefeller remained calm and collected under the pressure and the threats that the Pennsylvania Railroad was putting forth. Instead of opting to jump ship, like so many refineries were doing under such threats and uncertainty, he instead decided there was no better time than the present to spring to action. He quickly arranged a meeting with a man by the name of Jay Gould, a railroad magnate, and implemented a secret, confidential agreement that would ultimately establish and construct the Alleghany Transportation Company, which was described as "the first major pipeline networking serving Oil Creek."

Rockefeller and Flagler additionally would negotiate deals with the New York Central Railroad, whereby Rockefeller and partners made several agreements including assuming liability for any fires or accidents that may occur during transportation of products, agreeing to cease transportation via water routes during the summer months, and to transport at least 60 train carloads of refined oil each day. Though 60 carloads of oil was significantly more than Rockefeller's refineries were generating at that time, Rockefeller was planning on working alongside other oil refineries in Cleveland to make up for the difference. Per acceptance of these agreements, the New York Central railroad would go on to agree that they would, in turn, transport the crude oil from the Pennsylvania oil regions to Kingsbury Run and then take the refined oil from the Cleveland oil refineries to New York for only $1.65 a barrel, which was a huge savings as the typical going rate for this type of service was $2.40 at that time.

This arrangement would go on to be called the "Lake Shore Deal," and it would mark a significant turning point for how business should be done in America and also would take Rockefeller's finances to unmatchable numbers. The railroad industry would also come to understand just how well economies of such great scale could work to their own personal advantage. Therefore, they would also begin promoting monopolies of virtually all of the commodities that were being sold within the United States. It was the turning point in Rockefeller's career where future historians would go on to note that instead of simply being a highly intelligent young man with an incredible knack for business, he would be known as a man who was nothing short of a selfish crook who would stop at nothing to build his business to unmatchable success, including making it virtually impossible to small businesses to find success while setting about attaining all of the wealth and fortune that he possibly could.

It is of great importance to make note of the fact that railroad rebates were given to large businesses following the Civil War as a means to assist in recouping the losses that prevalently hit the railroads during the war. By the end of the 19th century, however, railroad rebates would come to be considered nothing more than a cheap scheme, yet they would continue to be a standard business practice in 1872. It would not be until 1887 and the implementation of Interstate Commerce Act when railroad rebates would technically become illegal for distribution and use. However, it would not be until 1903 when they would be eliminated entirely. The underlying basis for this was due solely to the fact that railroads were granted eminent domain so that they could successfully spread across the United States. In other words, railroads were fully capable of being able to drive landowners out and force them to sell their land to the railroads so they could build more railroad tracks across the country. Usually, such practices are limited to organizations who have the common good in mind, however, during these years, land was basically nothing more than simply available for the taking by the highest bidder. These tactics are now considered unethical for large companies, which have already been granted special deals and rights to set about making secretive deals behind closed doors for their own benefit. However, back in 1872, it was purely uncharted territory in both law and business, and the act of making monopolies illegal along with holding big businesses accountable for unethical practices are what came about following such unlawful practices of the 19th century.

In 1874, Rockefeller met in private with two men by the names of William G. Warden and Charles Lockhart. They were the heads of two of the largest oil refineries in Philadelphia and

Pittsburgh. He met them in order to share all of the benefits that they could potentially receive if they joined with the Standard Oil Company. Rockefeller would use his standard method of showing the men Standard Oil Company's books so that they could see firsthand the actual evidence of the company's profit margin. Even in the middle of a depression, the Standard Oil Company was doing so well financially that they could easily have slashed their prices to below the operation costs of firms that were located in Pennsylvania and could still successfully turn a profit. The two men were quite obviously inspired, and virtually overnight, Standard Oil Company had successfully taken over more than half of the oil refineries in Philadelphia and Pittsburgh and would soon take over the rest, making sure that he targeted all of the oil refineries that laid closest to the railroads as well.

Rockefeller then turned his sights to the Oil Creek region of Pennsylvania. This would prove to be a bit more trying for him to obtain. This was due to the fact that though oil was coming from Oil Creek in full abundance, the region itself was, from a financial standpoint, actually quite poor. Successfully building and operating oil refineries would prove quite daunting as the cost of shipping supplies and chemicals over the incredibly rigid terrain of the area would be incredibly expensive and hard to accomplish. The people of Oil Creek were also incredibly possessive of their oil. While Rockefeller viewed taking over the region as nothing more than another bout of business he needed to attend to, the people of Oil Creek felt as if he was infringing upon what God had given them, and they certainly did not feel obligated to share their black gold with a greedy, money-hungry man. That is precisely why the residents of Oil Creek felt as if they had been utterly and completely betrayed when the owners of the Imperial Refining Company (Oil Creek's very own principle refinery) sold their oil refinery to the Standard Oil Company. It would also spark the final days of ending independent oil refining in the area; as soon after the purchase of Imperial Refining Company, the Standard Oil Company would also purchase the second largest oil refinery, and so on and so forth until it controlled every single one in Oil Creek.

One of the secret weapons that John D. Rockefeller implemented was that of a 27-year-old man by the name of John D. Archbold. Archbold was a former employee of the second-largest oil refinery in Oil Creek, and though he once vehemently condemned Rockefeller during many speeches that he had once given at various town halls and opera houses, Rockefeller took him under his wing, making him an ambassador for "Acme Oil Company," which was really just Standard Oil Company using a different name as a front. This significantly helped him to convince other refineries to follow suit without having to be scared off by the venomous name of the Standard Oil Company. Rockefeller was so incredibly impressed with how successful Archbold was that he entrusted him as his right-hand apprentice.

Rockefeller was quickly on his way to taking complete control of all of the major oil refineries in the United States. He was able to successfully maintain profitable relationships with three of the largest railroad lines that serviced the oil regions. This relationship made it simply not possible for independent oil refineries that were still refusing to join forces with the Standard Oil Company to transport their oil at better prices. However, there was a large void that remained in the map of the oil regions. That was the territory that was regulated by the B&O (Baltimore and Ohio) Railroad, and it was their tracks that expanded throughout the southern region of Pennsylvania. B&O's tracks in Pennsylvania also connected to a series of oil refineries throughout Wheeling and Parkersburg in West Virginia, not to mention having an oil export base in Baltimore, Maryland. In other words, all of the oil refiners who refused to team up with the Standard Oil Company were utilizing the services of B&O Railroad as opposed to any of the other railroads who were being backed by the Standard Oil Company.

Rockefeller found a way around all of this by going about secretly buying and ultimately renaming the biggest refining operation that the B&O Railroad served: J.N. Camden and Company. J.N. Camden was now the owner of the newly named Camden Consolidated Oil Company and took it upon himself to hide the fact that he had secretly collaborated with Rockefeller from B&O Railroad. In turn, he also began negotiations to receive the same rebates for his "new" refinery as the Standard Oil Company was receiving from the railroads they were utilizing to transport their own oil. Baltimore and Ohio Railroad's president still placed his confidence in the belief that he was holding his own against the Standard Oil Company and Rockefeller himself, whereby, he was actually working directly in their favor. J.N. Camden went on to purchase all of the oil refineries that were located in the Baltimore region using the money he was receiving from the Standard Oil Company and with the new Camden Consolidated Oil Company name. In May 1875, all of these purchases were finalized, and Rockefeller was referred to as "the sole master of American oil refining." This was quite a title due to the fact that crude oil had yet to have been discovered anywhere else in the world in terms of major repositories. Rockefeller had control of oil not only on a national level but on a global scale as well.

In April 1874, Rockefeller would begin the process of taking over the railroads with great success. Erie Railroad handed over total control to the Standard Oil Company of one of their terminals that was located in New Jersey in exchange for half of the Standard Oil Company's business and also for their assistance in refitting their oil cars as well. Similar arrangements were also made with the railroad New York Central not long afterwards, and yet again, this would lead to a domino effect with more railroads following suit to become controlled by Rockefeller. Rockefeller also had a jump start with regards to the idea of purchasing the oil tank cars before the railroads had the idea, and once they had the idea to implement them by replacing the old freight cars, the vast majority of cars were already owned by the Standard Oil Company. It was significantly more profitable for the railroad lines to transfer oil via tank cars instead of loading them into the barrels and then onto the freight cars, so the railroads were then willing to be able to go about leasing the tank cars from the Standard Oil Company in exchange for their highly beneficial mileage rebates.

Rockefeller went on to utilize his power of proposition to negotiate with the railroads to wheel and deal different terms that would put a final end to the Oil Creek refineries. The only true advantage that the Oil Creek refineries had over the refineries that were based in Cleveland was the fact that they were located in closer proximity to the oil wells, so therefore, the costs to transport the oil was significantly lower. At this point, Rockefeller was demanding that railroads put forth uniform rates for all oil that was to be shipped. In other words, oil that was being shipped anywhere, be it Cleveland or Pittsburgh, would be shipped at the same rate, regardless of the distance.

The Standard Oil Company would also eventually start the process of building their own pipeline system. This would prove to be an incredibly trying task at first. Pipelines were something that were already being implemented, albeit slowly and far from perfectly, and railroad owners had a solemn feeling that pipelines would prove to be the future if they were laid successfully and would ultimately put an end to oil refineries' heavy dependence upon them. Rockefeller, who was typically at the forefront of the development of modern technology, was actually on the sides of the railroads at the start, and he wanted to delay the takeover of pipelines for as long as he could in order to gain as much profit as he possibly could while he still could. However, when the Empire Transportation Company made their case in showing that pipelines were, in fact, the future for the transportation of crude oil, Rockefeller and the Standard Oil Company jumped on board and formed their very own pipeline structure called the American Transfer Company, whereby Rockefeller would also go on to buy a third interest in the company that ran the United Pipe Lines as well. Similar to before, the only resistance that the Standard Oil Company was met with lay in both West Virginia and also in Baltimore, which is where the B&O Railroad still remained an independent firm. However, by the year 1877, the Standard Oil Company bought nearly all of the refineries that were available in the Baltimore area, and Rockefeller, at only 38 years of age, would go on to control 90% of all of the oil that was produced in the nation.

Teamsters would fight tooth and nail against the Standard Oil Company; however, they were bound for failure as it was tremendously easier and cheaper for producers to simply send crude through a pipeline system versus sending it in wagons Rockefeller would go on to strike up an agreement with the Erie Railroad and take control of vitally important terminal facilities that were located in the New York harbor in exchange for taking control of the shipping of half of the Standard Oil Company's oil that was located on the Erie.

Throughout 1875, the Standard Oil Company would continue to buy up more firms and pipelines and would merge them into what would be referred to as the United Pipe Lines by 1877. Rockefeller and Flagler haggled deals with railroad lines with each line agreeing to carry a certain percentage: Pennsylvania Railroad would carry51%; the Erie21%; Baltimore & Ohio 9%; and the NY Central20%. They additionally attained certain allowances from the railroad lines for being "eveners." To simplify, Standard Oil Company was charged to make sure railroads would all receive their fair share of the deal.

Between 1875 and 1876, Johnson N. Camden (who would later become a West Virginia senator) secretly came into Standard Oil Company and would make the move to purchase all of the oil supply in West Virginia in order to pressure the independent refineries of Pittsburgh, and by 1876, Camden would gain virtually full control of the vast majority of the oil refineries in West Virginia. The following year, Standard Oil Company would buy the Pennsylvania-based Columbia Conduit Co. in order to gain control of its refineries and its pipelines. Columbia Conduit Co. made various attempts to circumnavigate the Pennsylvania Railroad in order to erect a pipeline that extended from the oil regions downward to the contemporary B&O railroad that was located in close proximity to Pittsburgh.

The Pennsylvania Railroad utilized armed guards in order to prevent Standard Oil from placing a pipeline underneath the right-of-way that was located just north of Pittsburgh. The Standard Oil Company would seize control over the vast majority of the equity of Empire Transportation Company, which was a subsidiary of Pennsylvania Railroad. Empire Transportation Company had its own line of terminals, tank cars, lake steamers, and pipelines in the New York harbor. Empire Transportation Company threatened Standard Oil Company for a short duration of time, however, Rockefeller would go on to cancel all of his shipments with Pennsylvania Railroad, cut prices, and build 600 new tank cars, thus catapulting the railroad and leaving them with no other option but to sell their assets to Rockefeller.

In 1878, Rockefeller would also go on to purchase Bostwick and Tilford, which was one of the chief firms that dealt with refined oil, from a man named Jabez A. Bostwick. Bostwick and his ties to Long Island and New York harbor oil facilities would be brought on board to join the Standard Oil Company. The following year, Standard Oil would go on to acquire Long Island-based Devoe Manufacturing Company along with Chess, Carley, and their ties to vital distribution systems that were located in the Louisville, Kentucky, region.

Between 1877 and 1878, Standard Oil Company and the trunk lines would move forward with a new arrangement in terms of splits with New York City holding 63%, Pennsylvania Railroad holding 47%, Philadelphia and Baltimore holding 37% each, Erie and NY Central holding 21% each, and B&O holding 11% of total traffic. By 1878, Standard Oil would force railroads to have to pay a drawback fee of twenty cents to thirty-five cents per barrel of crude oil if it was shipped by a non-Standard Oil party. This combination of drawbacks and rebates are what would inevitably force all of the remaining independently-owned refiners to eventually cave in and join Standard Oil Company. Production would go on to increase in the oil regions of Pennsylvania due to the abundant discovery of oil in the Bradford region, and Standard Oil was left no other option but to desperately construct as many sizable holding tanks as they possibly could in order to take hold of the market's oversupply of oil. By the year 1879, Standard Oil Company was doing 90% of all of the oil refining within the United States alone and nearly 70% was exported overseas. Business became so complex and in such full abundance that Rockefeller would find himself only being forced to deal with major issues and larger details of business affairs, all at the age of only 40.

By 1879, the Standard Oil Company was laying upwards of a mile and a half of new pipeline each and every day in the oil regions, which truly was an astounding amount given the fact that all of the work was completed via manpower. When new oil wells were struck, a Standard Oil Company representative would arrive on the doorstep of the oil well's owner and would try and strike a negotiation to have the option to connect their oil well directly to one of the pipelines. If they agreed, they would be financially secure for the rest of their life. However, due to the fact that as the Standard Oil Company controlled all of the oil pipelines within the region, and oil was only worth anything if it was connected to a pipeline, oil well owners were financially dependent on the rates that Standard Oil opted to pay. Unfortunately, for those who decided not to join forces with the Standard Oil Company, they would find that no profit of any sort would ever come their way. Interestingly, the resentment levels against Rockefeller and the Standard Oil Company were so high that the oil well owners who resided in Titusville, PA, went on to develop what would be called the "Petroleum Parliament" in order to be able to meet and talk about various plans to construct two brand-new independently owned pipelines that would lead eastward towards the Atlantic Ocean. By this point in time, the longest pipeline only covered 30 miles, and between the years of 1879 to 1883, Standard Oil Company would see only one serious competition arise. The Tidewater Pipe-Line Company (later called the Tidewater Oil Company) would take Rockefeller by complete surprise as they succeeded in constructing a pipeline from the oil regions eastward across northern Pennsylvania and into Williamsport. This specifically was the region where oil was being transported to the Reading Railroad. Reading then set about transporting the oil to an oil refinery that was located in Chester,

Pennsylvania, along the Delaware Bay. While Rockefeller ultimately would go about making multiple attempts to take control over Tidewater, he would ultimately fail, and on May 28 of 1879 Tidewater Pipe-Line Company would successfully complete construction of their pipeline. The pipeline pumps were initiated at their point of origin, which was located in Bradford, PA, and it would take a week for the oil to pass over the region's mountains and rugged landscape at a significantly greater distance and length than anyone had thought was previously possible. Oil would flow into the point of termination with great success, much to the dismay of Rockefeller and the whole of the Standard Oil Company.

The man who had coordinated the Oil Creek pipeline construction for Standard Oil Company, Daniel O'Day, wanted desperately to physically destroy the Tidewater pipeline, however, Rockefeller out and out refused to lower himself to such levels. Rockefeller instead went on to reduce rates that were being charged by Standard Oil's pipelines while also having the railroads lower their rates for the use of their oil tank cars. They kept rates so incredibly low that they were hardly even making a profit. This drove Tidewater to undercut their services to the point where they were merely operating at half their capacity. Rockefeller, however, would end up being met with the ultimate surprise. The man who was running Tidewater Oil Company, Byron Benson, went on to tell Mr. O'Day that he wanted to "let the bar down" and that he believed that the time had finally come for the two companies to work together as opposed to against each other in order to prevent other oil companies from attempting to take over. This, of course, came as a striking blow to the oil regions who had viewed Tidewater Oil Company as their only want to remain liberated from the Standard Oil Company. However, it was something that was imminent at some point in time. Byron Benson allowed the representatives from the Standard Oil Company to buy up a minority stake in Tidewater, and in 1883, both of the companies came to a final agreement with the Standard Oil Company taking 88.5% of all of the pipeline business and the Tidewater Oil Company taking the remaining 11.5%.

Standard Oil would continue to grow, thus spreading to different states, and in turn, the company would soon control 90% of oil refineries across the United States. At this point in time, however, oil refiners and well owners began to get a bit unnerved with regards to the looming threat of oil ever running dry in the country. By this point in time, Pennsylvania was still the only crude oil deposit in the world, which was largely why there were such concerns as to it eventually running out. Rumors swirled about possible crude oil being found in Russia, but Rockefeller had devoted his entire career to building his oil empire in the United States. Even if the Russians had found oil, he would have been less than willing to pay the prices that they would have been required to pay in order to access it. His luck would change in 1885, when oil was struck in a region that was in close proximity to Lima, OH. Unfortunately, Ohio oil was not as good as Pennsylvania oil in terms of its chemical capacity, and even when it was refined, it gave off a foul-smelling sulfuric odor that led to it being labeled "skunk oil." Many oil refiners highly doubted that it could ever be refined so well that it could fetch the same prices as Pennsylvania oil, and many were quite apprehensive that the Ohio crude oil would even last for any extended period of time. Rockefeller, however, maintained that oil was a blessing from God, and this was yet another gift that was to be used for his full benefit. Rockefeller was by and large determined to invest in the Ohio crude oil, even to the point that though his associates at the Standard Oil Company blatantly refused to invest, Rockefeller took it upon himself to invest his own money, 3 million dollars, in the oil. He told his associates that if it didn't work out, it would be his loss. However, if it did, he was to be reimbursed by Standard Oil. Rockefeller's associates were so motivated by Rockefeller's sheer will and determination that they would ultimately go on to approve the investment as a company.

John D. Rockefeller was by and large a man of great faith; however, this faith was most certainly not blind. Rockefeller choosing to invest in the oil fields of Ohio was most certainly a risk, and it was one that he was not going to take without proceeding with caution. One of the first things that Rockefeller opted to do was to hire one of the best chemists in the United States, Herman Frasch. Rockefeller provided him with all of the funds necessary as well as a state-of-the-art laboratory, and he gave Frasch only one job: to eliminate the foul odor by treating the crude oil. He also went about sending various teams that represented the Standard Oil Company to different hotels, factories, railroads, warehouses, and other businesses in order to put forth the thought that those industries should hop on board with the idea of using fuel oil in their furnaces as opposed to coal. Kerosene was the number one product that was being put forth by the oil that was coming from the Pennsylvania oil regions, and it was perfect for lighting up churches and homes because it did not put off any foul smells and was incredibly bright. However, if the Standard Oil Company could get these companies on board, the poorer quality and the smell was something that would not be noticed in industrial settings.

The risk that Rockefeller took was one that would certainly go on to pay off. Frasch was able to successfully remove the smell from the Ohio crude oil by utilizing copper oxide to remove the sulfur. Though the process left behind a little bit of residue, the oil itself could not have come at a better time. Pennsylvania was, in fact, being depleted of its crude oil, and while eventually Kansas and Texas would both explode onto the scene with their own black gold explosions, it would be a decade where the nation would rely solely upon the crude oil that came from the soil of Ohio alone.

The Standard Oil Company went on to buy approximately 300 acres of land in West Virginia and

Pennsylvania, and by the year 1891, the company owned the vast majority of land in the oil fields of Indiana and Ohio as well. The Ohio oil fields were quite vast and stretched out for over 100 miles, and the flatter land of the Midwest region made the area significantly more accessible than that of the difficult terrain of Pennsylvania; and that in particular was incredibly beneficial as constructing oil refineries in the area was something that was faster and easier to do, which saved the Standard Oil Company from having to ship the crude oil back east and then back to the Midwest again for sales.

Rockefeller was now a successful millionaire. However, Standard Oil was so large and spread out that it was purely impossible for him to control every aspect of the company on his own, so he permitted all of the former oil refinery owners that he had previously bought out to serve as his board of trustees. He was now the head of the most intelligent group of oil refinery experts in the world. While this is something that is not very new with regards to the confines of our modern-day society, such a board of directors was simply unprecedented at the time of Rockefeller's years of reign, and this would set the stage for how future companies should be run in order to obtain true wealth, success, and power.

The 19th century was at the epitome of the Industrial Revolution and with that was the significant need for the railroad. This was literally the very first time throughout history where large cargo could be transported across the country and everywhere in between with such speed and success. By the 1860s, the two largest industries in the United States were, of course, the oil industry and the railway industry. And that makes it no great surprise that John D. Rockefeller wanted to have his hands in both worlds.

His ultimate plan was to basically do precisely with the railroad industry what he had done with regards to taking over the oil refinery industry, and he was already in close talks with the Vanderbilt family. He was also in talks with countless railroad owners in order to purchase their stocks and strike deals to ultimately take over. He had to gain the trust of the presidents of the railroads so that he could secure a beneficial deal with them to transport his oil at the best prices possible. He successfully negotiated with the Pennsylvania Railroad to get a super-discounted rate on the shipping of his oil.

This relationship lasted for quite a while until 1877 when the Pennsylvania Railroad spent an overwhelming amount of money to expand their railway system and found that they could no longer match Rockefeller's discount at the rate in which it would have been beneficial to them. In fact, if they would have continued the discount, it potentially could have bankrupted the company entirely. Therefore, they raised their prices, thus going back on their agreement with Rockefeller. Instead of getting angry, Rockefeller took it upon himself to lay his own system of underground pipelines. He reached out to other railroad companies, and the Pennsylvania Railroad simply lost their biggest and best customer as well as their largest source of income.

As Rockefeller was the main controller of the oil in the country, this outraged him and led him to storm in on the Pennsylvania Railroad executives, exclaiming that what they were attempting to do was "nothing less than piracy!" And, to make matters even worse, railroad workers were claiming that they were not getting paid, which was leading to strikes across the United States. This would ultimately lead to what is most commonly referred to as "The Great Railroad Strike" of 1877. Buckling under the pressure, Pennsylvania Railroad gave in and sold their oil refinery company to Rockefeller for a whopping $3.4 million.

Attorney Samuel Dodd thought that setting up a trust for the company would be in their best interests, and with that, the Standard Oil Trust was established on January 2, 1882. The Standard Oil Company Board of Trustees was assembled, and all of the properties of Standard Oil Company were situated in the hands of the members. Each stockholder was to receive 20 Certificates of Trust for each of the shares they owned in Standard Oil stock. All of the profits from integral companies were to be provided to the nine trustees who were in charge of determining the dividends for the company (these trustees were also in charge of electing the officers and the directors of those very sam

component corporations as well). The Standard Oil Trust wa

capitalized at quite a conservative value of $78 million, howeve

the actual value of the Trust was roughly $200 million. Thos

nine Trustees alone were in charge of 23,314 of the total 35,00

shares, with Rockefeller holding 9,585 of them. At the age of 4:

Rockefeller was considered the first amongst his peers and thu

he was deemed the leader of the Standard Oil Trust. Thoug

Rockefeller was put in charge of the Trust of the company, he sti

could not seize total control of the policy regardless of h

personal feelings.

In 1887, the United States government would go on t

pass the Interstate Commerce Act, the first transportatio

regulation commission. The Interstate Commerce Act force

regulations on the prices charged by railroads, which prevente

price gouging by railroad companies for the use of transportatio

It was this act that would ultimately end up making railroa

rebates illegal once and for all. The Standard Oil Company woul

go about making a very public acknowledgement of the act an

vowed that they would abide by the new regulation an

henceforth would no longer go about accepting the railroa

rebates. Much to the contrary, however, for a number of yea

their trust had been going around many of the similar laws tha

states were trying to implement. One of the top representatives o

the Standard Oil Company, Col. W.P. Thompson, would go on t

explain how all of this was being taken care of to Rockefelle himself, stating that their "arrangement is a very simple one: we are paying the open tariff rates to Michigan and all other points, and this is required of all other shippers. I have a distinct understanding with the proper persons that we are not required or expected to pay more than formerly and in order that we may not be out any money… we deduct from Chicago payments an equivalent amounting to what would have been a proper payment on all the other points, each month. You will readily see the object of this and you will observe in the situation we are in that no better or fairer arrangement could possibly have been made or one more satisfactory to us." The Standard Oil Company owned a huge fleet of the oil tank cars that the railroads heavily relied upon as the main source of their business, and the railroad lines simply could not could not have afforded to lose their relationship and reliance on Standard Oil, at least not until more firm regulations could be set in place and followed with success, and that is something that would not occur until the start of the 20th century.

At the same time, the citizens of the United States, however, failed to see that the railroad system had broken a contract, but they deemed Rockefeller a villain of sorts, believing that he simply had significantly too much power. They saw Rockefeller as an enemy who would eventually take over the railroad system as he did the oil industry and would continue to keep taking until there was virtually nothing left for the taking for anyone else, particularly small businesses.

By 1890, Standard Oil Company had developed a detailed distribution system that would reach virtually every town in America, and by 1904, at least 80% of towns in the United States were supplied by Standard Oil Company's carts, which set about delivering various commodities directly to homes and businesses alike. Standard Oil Company's movement to overshadow retail markets of even the smallest sizes is easily the most crucial cause that led to Standard Oil Company becoming so heavily resented by the American people as a whole. Standard Oil was incredibly domineering in their marketing strategies. They even went about attempting to demand that all hardware and grocery stores that sold lubricants and kerosene sell nothing other than products that were made by Standard Oil. Though this policy was successful for a short duration of time, it would go on to only further increase the American public's disdain for Standard Oil Company and significantly increase the company's susceptibility to politically-based attacks.

Rockefeller and the Standard Oil Company were successfully taking over both the oil industry and the railroad industry, and this was truly alarming. Red flags were being raised throughout the nation about the need for something to be done in order to put a stop to such a complete takeover. In fact, President Teddy Roosevelt himself swore that he would do something to stop antitrust and to prevent this sort of takeover from happening. The state of Ohio went about setting in motion a variety of antitrust laws in order to stop Standard Oil and Rockefeller (specifically) from having a monopoly and ultimately taking over the entire industry. As this was only a state law in Ohio at the time, Rockefeller decided to reincorporate his business in New Jersey (with headquarters on Broadway in New York City, New York) in 1882. He accomplished all of this before the state of Ohio even had the opportunity to try and sue him. While this reincorporation worked for the time being, by 1890, Congress had passed the Sherman Antitrust Act, thus making such takeovers illegal in every state.

On March 21,1892, the Supreme Court made the decision that Standard Oil violated the law and demanded that the Standard Oil Trust be formally dissolved. Each trust certificate was to be exchanged for the proportional share of stock in the 20 component companies of the Standard. However, Rockefeller found a loophole in the system. The irony is that this had no practical effect on the Combination. The same men were still in charge, only now, they were simply the majority shareholders of all the component companies. The Board of Trustees from Standard Oil divided amongst themselves, in turn, creating smaller oil companies, which meant that they could not be considered a monopoly. By 1899, all of the companies were again brought back together under Standard Oil Company as subsidiaries (Chevron, Exxon, and BP are just a few examples of these subsidiaries that are still around).

Chapter Four:
Ida Tarbell and the Muckrakers

Muckrakers were journalists during the Progressive Era (1890s to 1920s) in the United States. These reform-minded people took it upon themselves to expose leaders who they felt were corrupt, as well as well-established corporations. Today, we consider these types of journalists to be investigative journalists or watchdog journalists. Muckrakers tended to have large followings of people who read more popular, trending magazines of the time and grew increasingly popular for their success in exposing magnates and ruthless corporations. With such rising growth in terms of the popularity of exposing such corruption and the people involved in corruption in the United States, it really was no great surprise that John D. Rockefeller's name would eventually come across the drawing board of these journalists.

It was the Cleveland Massacre where a number of red flags had been raised in the eyes of the muckrakers. However, in November 1902, a woman by the name of Ida Tarbell wrote a 19-part serial exposé in *McClure's Magazine,* entitled "History of Standard Oil Company," in which Rockefeller's public reputation was on the line. The expose proclaimed that he was a man fueled by nothing more than corruption and greed. There had been a number of unauthorized biographies about John D. Rockefeller by this time and throughout his lifetime. All of the biographies had one thing in common. They were all quite flattering and entirely uncritical towards Rockefeller. Additionally, they spoke volumes as to giving way to the boastful ideology of one becoming a self-made millionaire, and they spoke less to the methods that the man behind the money used in order to obtain that much money and success. Furthermore, none of them shed any light on the family who created the man that would become the wealthiest man in the world. There was no mention of the schemes that were conducted by his snake-oil selling, bigamist of a father, and they also failed to mention all of the schemes that were implemented by the Standard Oil Company in order for them to utterly wipe out their competitors and become what would be known as the company who was the "mother of monopolies."

In the expose, she would go on to name a number of issues and ordeals that Rockefeller went through and also the atrocities that he enacted in order to achieve success. In one of the articles, she went on to discuss the effect that he had on the oil industry at the time that he had successfully taken over his own firm. "In the new firm Andrews attended to the manufacturing. The pushing of the business, the buying and the selling, fell to Rockefeller. From the start, his effect was tremendous. He had the frugal man's hatred of waste and disorder, or middlemen and unnecessary manipulation, and he began a vigorous elimination of these from his business. The residuum that other refineries let run into the ground, he sold. Old iron found its way to the junk shop. He bought his oil directly from the wells. He made his own barrels. He watched and saved and contrived. The ability with which he made the smallest bargains furnishes topics to Cleveland storytellers today. Low-voiced, soft-footed, humble, knowing every point in every man's business, he never tired until he got his wares at the lowest possible figure. 'John always got the best of the bargain,' old men tell you in Cleveland today and wince though they laugh in telling it. 'Smooth, and a savvy fellow,' is their description of him. To drive a good bargain was his way of life."

The narrative that Tarbell put out was able to successfully expose all of the various components of Rockefeller's tactics to stomp out the competition, and it also went on to bring to light all of the domination and domineering tactics that were utilized by the Standard Oil Company within the confines of the oil industry. Ida Tarbell's installments would eventually go on to be published as a book that boasted the same name as the original exposé, and the book itself quickly rose to the charts to become a bestseller. The spotlight shone on the business tactics of Rockefeller and Standard Oil would become harshly attacked not only by the media but by federal and state courts as well.

This work by Ida Tarbell would go on to contribute to the disintegration of the monopoly of Standard Oil and, in turn, drive the Clayton Antitrust Act forward. Her work would additionally lead to the passage of the Hepburn Act in 1906 to oversee the railroads, the 1910 Mann-Elkins Act that gave the Interstate Commerce Commission power over oil rates, and the creation of the Federal Trade Commission (FTC) in 1914. She was a pioneer who was the very first person, man or woman, who took it upon herself to dive head-first into the lives of the men who had built a company as vast and successful as the Standard Oil Company in order to pull out all of the information that the men endured in order to make the firm reach such levels of greatness and expose some of the nasty methods that they had used in order to fulfill and reach those goals.

In 1901, Tarbell, who was working as a desk editor at the time, would go on to turn that position to a man named Lincoln Steffens and would throw herself into investigating the Standard Oil trust along with the assistance of her assistant, John Siddall. Tarbell opted to research Standard Oil, largely due to the fact *McClure's Magazine* had already set in motion the stages for exposing all of the wrongs that were occurring in American society at the time, and Standard Oil was the prime example to expose. The magazine had most recently gone about publishing a series on American crime. Editors, including Tarbell, were desperately seeking another story to break the headlines.

McClure editors finally settled upon exploring the growth of trusts in America, and while the sugar and steel industries were considered, it was Tarbell who volunteered the idea of American oil trust, as she had her own firsthand experiences in the oil fields of Pennsylvania. Moreover, a red flag was raised that the Standard Oil trust was represented only by Rockefeller, which would assist in ensuring that the story would be one that would be easy to follow. Ida traveled to Europe where she met personally with S.S. McClure in order to sell the idea to him. He had been staying in Europe to recover from exhaustion, however, this idea for a series of such articles would go on to kick him back into gear. The two would go on to discuss ideas over the course of several days in Milan at a spa. Upon Ida's return to the United States, Samuel Clemens (or as he is more popularly known, Mark Twain), would introduce her to the Vice-President of the Standard Oil Company, Henry H. Rogers, who was the third man in charge of the trust after William Rockefeller and John D. Rockefeller himself.

William Rogers first launched his career in the same area of western Pennsylvania where Ida was raised. Rogers and his partner were a pair that Rockefeller had initially bought out, and shortly thereafter, Rogers would join the Standard Oil Company trust. In 1902, Tarbell would begin conducting interviews with Rogers. He tended to be quite a guarded man when it came to issues that were related to finances and business, particularly with regards to Standard Oil. However, Tarbell put off the persona that the articles she was working on would be complementary to the corporation and the men who ran it. The two would meet several times at the headquarters of Standard Oil and Rogers was more often than not quite forthcoming in his interviews. Little could he have known that the interviews he was giving to Tarbell were formulating a negative exposé regarding the unfavorable business practices of Rockefeller and Standard Oil as a whole.

Ida Tarbell would also go on to describe in such intricate detail the evolution that the oil regions of Pennsylvania undertook in the way of crude oil being refined into kerosene. She stated, "twelve years before this strip of land had been but little better than a wilderness; its chief inhabitants the lumbermen, who every season cut great swaths of primeval pine and hemlock from its hills, and in the spring floated them down the Allegheny River to Pittsburgh. The great tides of Western emigration had shunned the spot for years as too rugged and unfriendly for settlement, and yet, in 12 years, this region avoided by men had been transformed into a bustling trade center where towns elbowed each other for place, into which three great trunk railroads had built branches, and every foot of whose soil was fought for by capitalists. It was the discovery and development of a new, raw product, petroleum, which had made this change from wilderness to marketplace. This product in 12 years had not only peopled a wasted place of the earth, it had revolutionized the world's methods of illumination and added millions upon millions of dollars to the wealth of the United States."

In addition to her interviews with Rogers, Standard Oil executives, its competitors, academic experts, and government regulators, she also took on the task of investigating Rockefeller and Standard Oil via documents and spent countless hours scouring through hundreds of thousands of documents that she collected that had been distributed across the United States. She was additionally able to locate a critical component of information that had mysteriously gone missing years before. It was a book entitled "The Rise and Fall of the South Improvement Company." Originally published in 1873, Rockefeller and Standard Oil were rooted in the illegal schematics of the South Improvement Company. The Standard Oil Company had made every attempt to destroy every copy of the book that was ever put into print, however, Tarbell finally stumbled across a copy of the book in the New York Public Library.

Ida Tarbell went on to discuss Rockefeller's initial tactics to establish total dominance over the oil refineries that were to be based in Cleveland, Ohio, stating that, "the chief refining competitor of Oil Creek in 1872 was Cleveland, Ohio. Since 1869, that city had done annually more refining than any other place in the country. Strung along the banks of Walworth and Kingsbury Run, the creeks to which the city frequently banishes her heavy and evil-smelling burdens, there had been since the early '60s from 20 to 30 oil refineries. Why they were there, more than 200 miles from the spot where the oil was taken from the earth, a glance at a map of the railroads of the time will show that by rail and water, Cleveland commanded the entire Western market. It had two trunk lines running to New York, both eager for oil traffic, and by Lake Erie and the canal it had for a large part of the year a splendid cheap waterway. Thus, at the opening of the oil business, Cleveland was destined by geographical position to be a refining center.

Ida also went on to provide pretty direct narratives of the lives of the men who ran the Standard Oil Company during its infancy of the firm's growth. She largely credits the important role that Samuel Andrews had in the early days of the firm, as compared to when Rockefeller took the reins in the latter, more successful days. She also notes that Rockefeller failed to give proper credit to the work that Andrews put forth, and she made note of the ever-important role that the younger Rockefeller, William, played in the growth and development of the Standard Oil Company, "Not only did Mr. Rockefeller control the largest firm in this most prosperous center of a prosperous business, he controlled one of amazing efficiency. The combination, in 1870, of the various companies with which he was connected had brought together a group of remarkable men. Samuel Andrews, by all accounts, was the ablest mechanical superintendent in Cleveland. William Rockefeller, the brother of John D. Rockefeller, was not only an energetic and intelligent business man, but he was a man whom people liked. He was open-hearted, jolly, a good storyteller, a man who knew and liked a good horse, not too pious, as some of John's business associates thought him, not a man to suspect or fear, as many a man did John. Old oil men will tell you on the creek today how much they liked him in the days when he used to come to Oil City buying oil for the Cleveland firm. The personal quality of William Rockefeller was, and always has been, a strong asset of the Standard Oil Company." She then went on to state, "Probably the strongest man in the firm after John D. Rockefeller was Henry M. Flagler.

He was, like the others, a young man, and one who, like the head of the firm, had a passion for money and in a hard, self-supporting experience, began when a boy had learned as well as his chief, some of the principles of making it. He was untiring in his efforts to increase the business, quick to see an advantage, and quick to take it. He had no scruples to make him hesitate over the ethical quality of a contract that was advantageous. Success, that is, making money, was its own justification. He was not a secretive man like John D. Rockefeller, not a dreamer, but he could keep his mouth shut when necessary, and he knew the worth of a financial dream when it was laid before him. It must have been evident to every businessman who came in contact with the young Standard Oil Company that it would go far. The firm itself must have known it would go far. Nothing could have stopped the Standard Oil Company in 1870 with the business being what it was but an entire change in the nature of the members of the firm, and they were not the kind of material that changes.

Yet another break in the case would come from within the walls of the Standard Oil Company itself. It was this break in the story that would go on to prove that Standard Oil was, in fact, still utilizing both shady and all-out illegal practices. This came in the way of an office boy who worked at the headquarters of Standard Oil and whose sole job was to destroy any and all records that contained any sort of evidence that the railroad companies were sharing advance information about the shipments of oil refineries with Standard Oil executives. This, of course, would grant them the capabilities to simply undercut the oil refiners. The young worker just so happened to take note of the fact that the name of his Sunday school teacher, who was a refiner, was listed on several of the documents. He passed along the documents to his teacher, who then gave them to Tarbell to use in 1904.

The Standard Oil expose series launched in November 1902 in the McClure's Magazine issue, and it would continue for nineteen damning issues. Ida was fastidious in profiling the early development of Rockefeller's interest in oil as well as how the oil industry began in the first place as well as many of the countless, shady tactics that were used by Rockefeller to build the Standard Oil Company. When the series concluded, Tarbell also penned a profile of Rockefeller, which is believed to be the first-ever profile of a CEO. Ida Tarbell virtually, singlehandedly invented what we now know as investigative journalism, which is a form of journalism that was nonexistent at the turn of the century.

Though the very mention of the name Ida Tarbell would bring about an incredibly angry glare to the eyes of John D. Rockefeller, he simply could not refute the words that she had written. He simply dismissed her and often referred to her works as nothing more than rambling words from a "poison tongue." Though he was certainly unhappy with the works of Tarbell, she had successfully uncovered a large number of underlying and quite revealing facts as to the history and the juicy behind-the-scenes details of the Standard Oil Company and John D. Rockefeller. For example, when the oil industry was separated into competing encampments (i.e., the large New York and Cleveland oil refineries versus the Pennsylvania Oil Regions), Rockefeller, in turn, would find himself utterly holding tight to his oil refineries that were located on Kingsbury Run. His reasoning behind this was for a very good reason. Taking the oil from the oil wells to the oil refineries was the most costly and unsettling part of the business. Owners of wells needed to take care of the transportation fees by themselves, and rarely did well-owners have enough horses and carts or wagons to transport the oil themselves, so they were forced to hire teamsters (wagon driving teams) to transport the oil directly to the oil refineries and/or railroads. Unfortunately, teamsters charged a pretty hefty price to transport products, which led to well owners seeking out other options to help save funds, and this would end up bringing about development of oil pipelines. However, the teamsters would destroy as many of the oil pipelines as they could in order to secure the demand for their services. Though oil pipelines would eventually take over in terms of transporting oil, up until that point the oil refineries were able to wheel and deal in order to get the best price.

This was precisely why Kingsbury Run was so vitally important to the earliest successes of Rockefeller. Three of the top railroad lines were located in close proximity to Kingsbury Run, they were: the Erie Railroad, the Pennsylvania Railroad, and the New York Central; all of which were pining for Rockefeller's business, as it was his oil refinery that was producing at least double the amount of barrels that competing oil refineries were putting out. Furthermore, Rockefeller was able to bypass the spring months in which the thaw led to significant slow-downs in terms of transporting oil to the refineries, this was due to his capability to be able to transport crude oil via waterway of the Erie Canal. This placed him in a prime position to be able to successfully negotiate lower rates from the railroad lines, which every other oil refinery owner was simply unable to accomplish. Tarbell would further investigate this particular tactic, and when she went about interviewing Rockefeller's competition, 40 years after the fact, she found that these owners had gone to the railroads to demand the same rebates that Rockefeller was receiving, and they were promised that they would receive them as well, and they never did.

When Rockefeller was in his 90s, he was interviewed by a journalist, William O. Inglis, who shared with him the fact that Ida Tarbell had incriminated him by stating that some of the measures he took to achieve success included "threatening to crush rivals who refused to join his cartel" back in 1872. Upon listening to such an accusation, Rockefeller was furious, and Inglis went on to describe what happened next. " 'That is absolutely false!" exclaimed Mr. Rockefeller so loudly that I looked up from my notes. As he spoke, he jumped up from the big chair in which he was reclining and walked over to the table. His face was flushed, and his eyes were burning. It was the first time I had ever seen him show anything but pleasant feelings, and there could be no doubt that he was aflame with anger and resentment. His voice rang out loud and clear. He did not beat the desk with his fist but stood there with his hands clenched, controlling himself with evident effort. 'That is absolutely false!' he cried, 'and no man was told that by me or any of our representatives. You may put that down once and for all. That statement is an absolute lie.' " That accusatory statement truly struck a powerful chord with Rockefeller, and he would again bring it back up later in the interview with Inglis stating, "How ridiculous all that talk is! It's twaddle, poisonous twaddle put out for a purpose. As a matter of fact, we were all in a sinking ship, if existing cutthroat competition continued, and we were trying to build a lifeboat to carry us all to the shore. You don't have to threaten men to get them to leave a sinking ship in a lifeboat."

Though Rockefeller failed to have any sort of conscious regarding his actions that took place back in 1872 or the years that followed, it was the utter secrecy that surrounded his actions that were quite revealing in terms of those who were aware of what was taking place, and had no one uttered a word against Rockefeller. In fact, the majority of the deals that Rockefeller made, including that of the rebate deal he struck with the railroads, were not even set to paper, but only that of a handshake to seal the deal. Rockefeller was also quite quick to give credit to Flagler as being the one who had struck the transportation deal on his own. This was a great way to give credit to his partner while also separating himself from the railroad rebates, which was the number one area of his which was the most susceptible to criticism.

Chapter Five:

His Private Life

John Davison Rockefeller was an incredibly private man, and therefore, attempting to dig up information on his personal life can be an excruciatingly daunting task. However, there are some personal facts of his life that are of notable importance, and as he always separated his business life from his personal life, this chapter will be devoted entirely to the little known facts about the very private life of John D. Rockefeller Sr.

Easily one of his most important private life events that took place would occur in 1864, when at the age of 25, Rockefeller would marry a woman by the name of Laura Celestia Spelman (September 9, 1839 – March 12, 1915), or simply, "Cettie" as she was known by her friends and family. Cettie was born in the town of Wadsworth, Ohio, to a man who was a Puritan descendant by the name of Harvey Buell Spelman and Lucy Henry. The couple had moved to Ohio from Massachusetts, and Harvey, a devoted abolitionist, was incredibly active within the Congregationalist Church, politics, and had strong ties to the Underground Railroad, as well. A well-to-do family, the Spelmans would eventually move to Cleveland, Ohio, where Laura, a devout Christian and the valedictorian at her and Rockefeller's high school, would meet and fall in love.

Cettie's family home served as a stop along the Underground Railroad, and they assisted in ferrying slaves to more northern territory in order to assist them in gaining their freedom. In fact, the Spelman home was so prevalent in their role in the Underground Railroad, that the infamous Sojourner Truth (abolitionist, suffragist, and preacher) once sought refuge there. Cettie once said that the only time she ever saw her mother cook a hot meal for dinner on a Sunday was when she would cook a hot dinner for refugees who were about to embark on the long journey to freedom in Canada. It was such a rarity for her mother to cook on Sunday as, according to their religious belief system, work was forbidden on the day of the Sabbath.

Cettie was fond of many of the things that refined young women of the time enjoyed, including literature, music, and art. She was also an unwavering first-wave feminist who was coming into her own as a woman and was quite inspired by women like Lucretia Mott and Elizabeth Cady Stanton, two women who had organized the Seneca Falls Convention, a convention that advocated for women's suffrage. She was also named valedictorian of her high school, and her acceptance speech was titled, "I Can Paddle My Own Canoe," and contained tidbits that included, "Chided men for depriving women of culture hypocritically blaming them for their dependency. But give women culture - let her thread the many paths of science - allow mathematics and exact thought on all subjects to exert their influence on her mind and conventions need not trouble her about her 'proper sphere.'" Cettie was a firm believer in a woman' unique ability to be able to make her own way in the world. This was a fact well-proven as when the Spelman family went about moving to Iowa, Cettie and her sister, Lucy, (or Lute, as she was fondly referred to by friends and family) stayed behind in Cleveland in order to be able to attend Oread Collegiate Institute, which was one of the first higher learning institutions based in the United States that allowed women to attend. At the Institute, Cettie was in charge of running the campus literary magazine. She would often write articles regarding, "the three aristocracies then ruling America - an aristocracy of intellect in New England, wealth in the Atlantic states, and blood in the South." She and her sister would also study music at the Cleveland Institute, and the two ladies would go on to become teachers. She heavily relied upon her small teacher's salary to make ends meet and stand on her own two feet, as her family was not in a well enough position to support her on their own. This was something that she far from resented, however, and she was ever-grateful to have been put in a position of independence as a woman of the time.

She was noted to have been so pleased with her success in terms of her career and independence that there was a point in her young life when being married was of simply no importance to her whatsoever. She and Rockefeller wrote each other on occasion during these years, and she once told her former music teacher, "I seem to have no anxiety about a life of single-blessedness, but a gentleman told me not long ago that he was in no particular rush to have me get married, but he hoped that in the multitude of my thoughts I would not forget the subject." She was quite well aware of Rockefeller's intentions, however, female teachers were only permitted to work if they were single, and at the time, if she were to say yes to a marriage proposal to Rockefeller, she would ultimately have to resign from her beloved teaching position.

It was somewhat of a custom for the men in the Rockefeller family to marry a woman who was above their own social status. And it was this fact that John was well aware of. In his eyes, his father and grandfather marrying above themselves only led to suffering, unhappiness and heartache for their wives. Though Rockefeller intended to marry a woman from a family that was wealthier and in significantly better community standing than his own, he wanted to first be financially worthy of the woman he chose to wed; he wanted desperately to prove to his future wife that he had made something of himself first and foremost. John made a pact with himself that when he was able to provide his wife with a sense of security in their future that he would marry. John never doubted in his mind that Cettie would be the one he would share his life with. Since the two were only 16 years of age, they had found a sense of comfort in one another. She had encouraged him to pursue all of his business endeavors in order to ultimately find success for himself in his future.

Throughout the years, the two would remain very good friends. Cettie's family, once quite wealthy, had lost it all in a bank collapse (they would eventually recover, but it was not the same as before), and Cettie would closely follow John's busines successes over the years. Cettie would remain incredibly guarded with regards to the man in whom she would choose to devote her life to. She wanted to marry a man who would provide not only her but her family as well with a sense of financial security, just in case they were ever to lose their fortune again. John did not see that as gold-digging, in any way, shape, or form, it simply went on to show just how much sense Cettie had for herself. The two were the perfect match for each other, and though they both knew it, John would not propose for nine years. It was during this nine-year period of time that it took John starting at Hewitt and Tuttle to becoming the head of his own successful firm, Rockefeller and Andrews at the age of only twenty-five years old.

As Rockefeller's firm began to successfully establish and grow his oil refinery in Cleveland, he would take Cettie out on long drives along the riverside and share with her all of the details of the firm's operations. She would share her opinions, and he listened intently with great respect and admiration of the woman by his side. In 1864, however, another suitor would threaten Rockefeller's relationship with Cettie, and he knew there was no better time than the present to make his proposal to her. In March 1864, he offered marriage to Cettie in a similar fashion as a business proposal, and she would accept, in a similar businesslike manner. He purchased her an extravagant diamond engagement ring that was more suited to show both Cettie and her family that he was serious about his relationship with her and that he was in a good place to care for her and the Spelman family as well. This gesture would prove more than ample for Cettie's parents, and the young couple were to be married only six months after the initial proposal in the home of the Spelman family. As he had successfully gotten his point of seriousness across with regards to Cettie's engagement ring, the wedding ring itself only set John back a mere $15.

The two were unwavering in their faith, and the vast majority of Cettie's social events involved their church, just as John's were. They were also both ardent with regards to abolitionism and promoting temperance. Though Cettie and John were both devout in their faith, the two had shared common interests as well, including music. The two, in their youth, would often play duets on the piano, and for a brief moment, John even considered becoming a pianist. There was always a tremendous amount of mutual respect between the two of them. He often consulted Cettie about her views and thoughts before he made business decisions, and he was once quoted as saying of his wife that, "Her judgement was always better than mine. Without her keen advice, I would be a poor man."

When he had to travel for business, he would write her love letters, including sentiments to the likes of, "What a blessing that I have such a good and true wife. How much I would give for wings to reach you tonight." The two would go on to have children of their own, Elizabeth "Bessie," Alice, Alta, Edith, and John Jr., though Alice would sadly pass away during infancy. Though he was infamously very busy, Rockefeller was very much a devoted family man. A loving father and devoted husband, he was a man who never took his family for granted.

In 1873, the Rockefeller family would move to Euclid Ave. in Cleveland, also famously referred to as "Millionaire's Row." Though he wasn't quite considered a millionaire just yet, he was close enough to have been able to afford a lovely home along one of the most beautiful avenues in the United States and certainly the most beautiful in Cleveland. The avenue was home to some of the earliest wealthy families of the era, and though the Rockefeller residence was not the most splendid along the street, he preferred it that way and purchased the home in order for it to be a fixer-upper that he could perfect to his liking. Luxuries truly did not mean much to Rockefeller. He wanted a large home with vast ceilings, a huge yard where he could build coach houses and stables and have the opportunity to be able to landscape his own stunning garden. He was an avid fan of horse racing; it has been said that the stables he built for his horses, Flash, Baron, Jesse, Trifle, and Midnight were even more spectacular than the residence itself.

Cettie and John settled into domestic bliss together on Euclid Ave. John was in no way like his father when it came to his relationship with his wife, and a short bit later, their children. John would come home to Cettie at the end of his long days and would devote his time to her alone. When the two of them wanted to socialize, they would often go to Philharmonic performances, and they enjoyed hosting dinner parties with friends from their church. The Rockefellers held tight to their temperance-based faith and values and refused to engage in drinking alcohol, nor would they go to a restaurant that served alcohol. This was something that was pretty uncommon in those days, which is particularly why the Rockefellers mainly kept to themselves and their friends who shared their same beliefs.

While it may certainly appear as if Rockefeller was purely a "workaholic," particularly during his early days of launching his business as well as his career and upon moving to the mansion on Euclid Ave., Rockefeller actually spent a good majority of his time at home with Cettie. He even went about installing a telegraph line that connected the office to his home so he could remain at home but still be able to be contacted in the event that he was needed. Rockefeller would claim in his later years that the secret to his success was simply balance. He rested often, paced himself, kept his energy levels up, preserved his health, and kept his mind cleared of unnecessary thoughts; a prescription that must have suited him just fine seeing as he would live a long life of well over 90 years of age.

The first child of John and Cettie would arrive in 1886 and they named her Bessie. Though she would be born while the Rockefellers were still living at their home on Cheshire Ave., the couple would have four more children while they were living in the mansion on Euclid Ave. Alice was born in 1869, though she would only live to see the age of 2. Then, three more came along between the years of 1871 and 1874: Alta, Edith, and John Jr. A of the children would be born under the care of the first female doctor in Cleveland, Dr. Myra Herrick. Dr. Herrick would also go on to open a free medical clinic for poverty-stricken women that was staffed entirely by female physicians, and the Rockefellers would be among the first chief financial supporters of the clinic.

John D. Rockefeller Sr. was by all accounts a wonderful father who doted upon his children. He spent as much time with his family as he possibly could, even taking on baby duties as needed, which was usually left to the woman during those years. He was known to be playful, soft-spoken, and patient with his children. He loved to perform tricks for them, teach them how to swim, skate on frozen ponds, row boats, ride bicycles (a new invention at the time), and ride horses as well. He was also known to be quite overprotective of his children, however. The children were basically confined to the home. They were not permitted to attend public school and instead had a governess who educated them at their home. They were permitted to have friends visit them at the mansion for a week or so at a time, however, they were not permitted to leave to visit their friends.

It was largely due to the unwavering faith of John and Cettie that the children were brought up in the way that they were. If the family was invited to a public social outing, such as a picnic, John was known to go to the park first in order to inspect the area for any alcohol or beer bottles as to not expose his children to such "worldly" experiences. When John once wanted to buy all of the children bicycles, Cettie adamantly spoke against it, saying that the children should only have one bicycle in order to teach them how to properly share. She also dressed the children only in hand-me-down clothing, and John Jr. actually had to wear dresses as a small child because he was the littlest of his older sisters. Rockefeller was firm with regards to teaching his children the importance of developing a strong understanding of finances and having good, strong financial instincts. So, as opposed to simply handing them a weekly allowance, he paid them a set rate depending on the chores that they were required to do.

One example of the methods that he used to teach his children financial understanding was during a time that one of his daughters was riding with him on a train and he leaned over to tell one of his colleagues, "This little girl is earning money already. You never could imagine how she does it. I have learned what my gas bills should average when the gas is managed with care, and I have told her that she can have for pin money all that she will save every month on this amount, so she goes around every night and keeps the gas turned down where it is not needed." He also made sure that his children never knew just how wealthy the family was until they were fully grown. He felt that it was his duty to learn the art of being thrifty, as this is how he had learned to find his own success from a very young age. He made sure that his children were never without anything that they needed, but when it came to things that they wanted, he made sure that they learned how to work for it and to save up for it.

Cettie and John's marriage would remain a harmonious one that was virtually free of disagreements and quarreling, Cettie herself would change from a young woman who campaigned for women's rights and her own career focus to becoming a woman whose life revolved solely around her husband and her children. She prided herself on bringing her children up with morally upright beliefs, and she wanted them to learn how to do things for themselves. The family easily could have afforded to hire an entire staff to help service the house, and though Cettie eventually would hire two maids to help, she still took on the vast majority of the housework herself along with the help of the children.

Cettie's sister Lute came to live with the family shortly after the Rockefellers were married, and she would help with the children a great deal. Unlike her sister, Lute was a bit more relaxed with regards to her former religious upbringing. The children learned far more of the world from their well-read and unrigid aunt than they ever did from either of their parents.

It is interesting to note that a Rockefeller biographer named Ron Chernow spoke to Rockefeller's family and asked them about his relationship with his father and family. Rockefeller's children and grandchildren asserted that he never spoke much about his father, and that he never permitted him to be a part of their lives. Chernow would eventually uncover the burial plot for William Rockefeller, however, it would show that he was buried under an alias, that of " Dr. William Levingston" in a small cemetery in Freeport, IL. It would appear as if John D.

Rockefeller purely wanted the memory of his father to be completely erased. He also ensured that his children and grandchildren would never be permitted to meet his half-sisters. In fact, his half-sisters never received any part of his fortune, as he did not consider them to be members of his family.

Between the years of 1891 and 1892, all of the evidence on the record goes on to suggest that John D. Rockefeller partially suffered from a nervous breakdown due to being overworked. Rockefeller would end up developing a health condition called alopecia that would cause him to lose all of his hair, including his eyebrows, and would inevitably suffer from poor health throughout the 1890s. Initially, he would attempt to hide his hair loss by wearing toupees, however, as he aged he decided it was best to simply allow people to see him in public as he was.

During the early 1890s, the wealth that Rockefeller had accrued had grown to such an abundant amount that he found himself faced with a significant issue: what he was to do with all of the money he had accrued over the years. To resolve this dilemma, it was during this time that Rockefeller had also gained significant confidence in a man named Reverend Frederick T. Gates. Gates was a clergyman and the director of the American Baptist Education Society. It was this society that would go on to establish the university. Gates would also become the philanthropic advisor and investment manager to Rockefeller from September of 1891 to 1923. At this time, Rockefeller was overrun with requests from both charities and individuals alike requesting funds and charities. Gates took it upon himself to remove the financial stress and burden while also overseeing all of the investments that Rockefeller was involved in. And it was these investments that were starting to become quite large in their own personal ways.

By 1896, Rockefeller had all but ceased heading into his office on a daily basis, and a year later, in 1897, he would officially retire at the age of 58. Though he would take part in certain management decisions and activities for another two years, by the year 1899, he would make no further attempts to make managerial decisions on behalf of Standard Oil Company.

John Archbold would take over the daily ins and outs of running and managing Standard Oil Company from the mid-1890s and on. He was a man who heavily frowned upon prominence and often would reach out to ask Rockefeller to continue asking him to remain as the president of Standard Oil Company in name only. Rockefeller made quite a mistake by not announcing his retirement to the public; this was largely due to his resistance to the enticement of exploiting the Standard Oil Company's near-monopoly situation by way of raising product prices "too" much.

Though the pricing policies that Rockefeller implemented did end up resulting in certain "monopoly profits" for Standard Oil Company, it should be noted that they in actuality were mild and quite fair. Archbold, however, did not see eye to eye with Rockefeller with regards to this particular matter, and he would set in motion raising product and service prices on an incredibly aggressive level, which led to the dividends rolling in. Unfortunately, as previously stated, Rockefeller had not announced that he had stepped down from Standard Oil Company, and this meant that the people blamed him solely, even though he had nothing to do with regards to management.

John D. Rockefeller Sr. would officially retire from his duties at the Standard Oil Company in 1897. He left the company in the trusted hands of his own son, John D. Rockefeller Jr. Standard Oil Company was sued yet again in 1911 for violating the Antitrust Act, and the company would be forced to again break off into several dozen smaller entities. In turn, Rockefeller Jr. would go about investing in all of these smaller companies, and this clever move on his part would go on to create even more wealth for the Rockefeller legacy (which is estimated to be roughly $300 to $400 billion to this very day).

Chapter Six:

Rockefeller's Retirement and

Contributions

From the middle of the 1890s up until Rockefeller's death in 1937, Rockefeller would ensure that all of the activities that he partook in were, in fact, quite philanthropic in nature. The fortune of Rockefeller would peak by 1912 at nearly $900 million, however, by the time mentioned, he had already allocated hundreds of millions of dollars from his personal fortune. And, in 1897, his son, John D. Rockefeller, Jr., would join Gates in assisting in managing his father's wealth full-time as well. John D. Rockefeller Sr., though commonly vilified, was actually an incredibly generous man with his money. During his lifetime, he was highly regarded as being one of the wealthiest men in the world, and though he was a wealthy magnate, he lived an incredibly unpretentious, quiet lifestyle and for the most part kept an incredibly low profile. Rockefeller would rarely attend the same social conventions that his peers and colleagues did, such as the theatre. Yet, he was adamant about giving back to his church (was firm on tithing 10% of his paychecks, since he was 6 years old, to his church) and his community. Following the dissolution of the Standard Oil Company, and with his image and legacy becoming quite tarnished, Rockefeller would start to give away millions of the billions of dollars that he had accrued over the years without hesitation.

One of the largest contributions that Rockefeller made was to one university in particular. As Rockefeller was largely the one who was responsible for the formation of the University of Chicago, he gave $35 million over the course of roughly 20 years. By 1932, however, the university alone would receive $75 million. Additionally, under the advice of Gates, in 1901, Rockefeller founded the Rockefeller Institute of Medical Research (which is now known as Rockefeller University) in New York. Within the labs of this university, a wide array of cures, causes, and preventative measures for diseases would come to be discovered. This was including, but not limited to, the identification of DNA as the main source of genetic matter and even the cure of meningitis. The Rockefeller Institute of Medical Research was set up due largely to the insistence of his son, Rockefeller Jr., and the total charitable gifts that Rockefeller made to the Institute were upwards of $50 million by the early 1930s.

In 1903, Rockefeller founded the General Education Board, which, in the 63 years of its operation, had gone on to disperse over $325 million to various schools, colleges, and universities throughout the United States. The General Education Board was entirely devoted to the principal focus of improving the quality of education across the United States. The efforts of the General Education Board included, but were certainly not limited to, a wide array of initiatives that were primarily focused on the public education system in the South as well as the overall advancement of medical education. John D. Rockefeller Sr. made an initial contribution of a million dollars to the organization; however, those contributions would quickly grow to $43 million by 1907. At this time, the donation total was the largest gift to ever have been made to any philanthropic organization in history.

The first project that was launched by the General Education Board was to send agents throughout the Southern region in order to survey, analyze, and then report back their findings on the conditions that were occurring in both white and black schools in order to be able to provide those schools with free professional advice on how those schools could improve education and instruction as a whole. In 1913, the General Education Board would be renamed the Rockefeller Foundation. In 1919, Rockefeller contributed more than $50 million to the Board in order to assist in raising academic salaries, which, during the years of the first World War, were frighteningly low, and by 1929, Rockefeller would transfer $235 million dollars to the foundation.

In 1909, Rockefeller went on to launch a public health program called the Rockefeller Sanitary Commission that was aimed to assist in preventing and ultimately curing Hookworm disease, which was an incredibly serious health problem within the southern states. Three major diseases plagued the southern region between the 19th and early 20th centuries: yellow fever, malaria, and hookworm. This was largely due to the fact that so many in the South simply lacked proper sanitary conditions, like access to running water and even bathrooms. And, with poverty and a hot, muggy climate, many people tended to walk barefoot, often in soil that was contaminated with feces. This allowed for contact with hookworm larvae. By the time the Rockefeller Sanitary Commission was put in motion, over 40% (approximately 7.5 million people) of the southern population in 11 different states was found to be infected with hookworm and had no knowledge of it.

The Commission would go on to educate Southerners on how hookworm spreads, how it can be treated, how sanitary outhouses should be built and the importance of wearing shoes by way of paying personnel to sponsor public education campaigns and lectures. They also provided widespread testing. The Rockefeller Sanitary Commission successfully educated and treated more than 400,000 people throughout the South, and by the time the campaign ended (1914), hookworm was not considered a health issue any longer. The Rockefeller Sanitary Commission would go on to successfully expand to become the Rockefeller Foundation International Health Division. The International Health Division truly gained notoriety for aiming its focus on advancing research for various diseases, such as malaria, the flu, typhus, and tuberculosis.

In 1909, the health of Cettie would begin to start to decline, and she became so incredibly weak that she would have to be confined to a wheelchair. She spent the vast majority of her time in bed resting. Even though her husband was a great financial supporter of the medical field and had unmatched access to a large number of some of the best healthcare providers in the United States, Cettie remained incredibly unwilling to receive any extra care. By this time, she was suffering from a number of various ailments, including shingles, sciatica, pneumonia, and pernicious anemia. Rockefeller remained an incredibly doting and loving husband to his wife, caring for her at whatever rate possible, while at the same time living in utter dread with the thought of losing his wife. Unfortunately, during these years Rockefeller found himself having to be away from his wife more than he had liked to be, often for several weeks at a time. He had homes in four different states and maintained a strict rotating schedule of visiting each of them seasonally. He did this due to the fact that, as he was considered to be a resident of New York and paid his taxes there, if he stayed too long at any of his other residences he feared he would be forced to end up getting caught paying taxes on all of the properties.

By 1913, Cettie would add congestive heart failure, lumbago, and pleurisy to her growing list of ailments, and her condition was declining so quickly that her doctors told Rockefeller that she should not be moved from their home on Euclid Ave. in Cleveland. Rockefeller opted to risk dealing with tax collectors to remain close to his wife's side in Ohio. The two would often go for carriage and vehicle rides and often would attend church at their beloved Euclid Ave Baptist Church, where they attended when they were young so many years before. On one particular occasion, Rockefeller was asked to speak to the church's congregation, to which he graciously accepted, keeping his eyes locked on Cettie the whole time. He said, "People tell me I have done much in my life. I know I have worked hard. But the best thing I ever accomplished and the thing that has given me the greatest happiness was to win Cettie Spelman. I have had but one sweetheart and am thankful to say I still have her."

Through it all, he would continue with his philanthropic deeds, and the same year (1913) Rockefeller, along with his son, John Jr. (as president), and Gates (as trustee) established the Rockefeller Foundation that was aimed to assist in fostering the overall well-being of women and men across the world. In the first year alone, Rockefeller would donate upwards of $100 million to the foundation. The Rockefeller Foundation has implemented aid to education, social and medical research, the arts, public health initiatives, scientific advancements, and a large number of countless other fields expanding the globe. By 1923 the Rockefeller Foundation was noted to have become the biggest grant-making foundation in the entire world, with Rockefeller being praised as the most benevolent philanthropist in the history of the United States.

In the early spring of 1915, Cettie passed away while John was in Florida at his home in Ormond Beach. He was at the breakfast table with his son, John Jr. and daughter-in-law, Abby, when he received two telegrams: one stating that she was close to death and the second saying that she had passed. Though the news was certainly not really a surprise, Rockefeller was hit hard with the heavy news, and his son would later go on to comment that it was the first time in his entire life that he had ever seen his father cry.

In 1930, with a nation that was crumbled by the Great Depression, Rockefeller, who was already in his 90s, developed Rockefeller Center, which was considered to be a "city within a city." The center created more than 40,000 jobs during construction and afterwards. Although John D. Rockefeller Jr. spent most of his life engaged in philanthropy, his single defining business venture was the creation of the "city within a city."

Rockefeller Center would officially open in May 1933 with a firm belief in the fact that art was something of an act of good citizenship. For example, the lobby of 30 Rockefeller Plaza would boast art that was decorated by well-accomplished European artists, Josép Maria Sert and Frank Brangwyn. Over the course of the first 10 years of Rockefeller Center's completion, the 22-acre complex would find itself bustling with excited new tenants such as the brand-new publication, *News-Week* (its original name) and the ever-popular French bookstore, Librairie de France, just to name a few. Throughout the decade of the 1930s, Rockefeller Center would continue to steadily improve, adding notable amenities such as the ice skating rink and some of which were purely by accident like the Christmas tree tradition that began in 1931. By the end of the decade in 1939, over 125,000 people found themselves visiting the infamous Rockefeller Center each and every day.

In 1918, the last gift that John D. Rockefeller would personally give was the Laura Spelman Rockefeller Memorial, which for a number of years had made a large amount of progress and strides in the field of the social sciences. This was a very special gift for Rockefeller as it was a way for him to leave behind his wife's legacy and all of her charitable causes. Another member of the Rockefeller family would also go on to pay tribute to Cettie on a more personal level. John Jr. named one of his children, a son, Laurance, after his mother.

As the years passed, Rockefeller would see less and less of his children and his grandchildren. The relationship with one of his daughters, Edith, would also prove to be continuously strained over the years as she had traveled to Europe in 1913 in order to find treatment for her depression. She received help from Carl Jung, who helped her come to understand some of her inner turmoil and a lot of the pain she had carried from her difficult and questionable childhood. She had held mixed emotions about her relationship with her father, and though the two had regularl corresponded with each other, their letters were always a mixture of love and frustration between the two. Edith returned to the United States in 1932 after finding out that she was suffering from breast cancer. She died in 1932 at the age of only 60, and she had never visited her father upon her return. The two had gone 20 years without seeing each other.

John would spend the last of his days at his Florida home, where he enjoyed investing in gold and the stock market. The stock market crash of 1929 had greatly hit the Rockefeller family,   and while the family remained comfortably secure from a financial standpoint, John was still quite nervous as to having lost so many millions during that time. As he continued to age, his family would notice a significant change in his personality. He became a man of great cheer and was always quite happy. He remained an avid golfer up until 1932, when he suffered from a severe cold that would end up playing a role in how many rounds of golf he could play at a time, and he would unfortunately give up the sport entirely.

In 1934, at the age of 95, he suffered from pneumonia, and though he would recover, it took quite a toll on his physical well-being. Though his body was starting to decline, his mind stayed ever-sharp. He would spend the last years of his life sitting on his front porch, soaking in the Florida sunshine, blanket across his lap, and his eyes twinkling. Though he could no longer physically go to church, he would often tune in to sermons on his radio on Sunday mornings. He would receive one last financial hurrah at the age of 96, when his life insurance policy paid him a whopping sum of $5 million. This was because only one in 100,000 people who were born in the same year as Rockefeller would live to reach the age that he did.

Though he strived from a young age to reach 100 years old, John Davison Rockefeller passed away on May 23, 1937, from a heart attack, a mere two months shy of his 98th birthday. His total estate was valued at $26,410,837. This is due to the fact that he had simply given the vast majority of his assets and property to the philanthropies that he felt the most passionate about, as well as to his son, John D. Rockefeller Jr. and some of his other heirs.

Rockefeller was an entrepreneur who was truly an agent of change in terms of his philanthropic ventures. Rockefeller clearly made successful changes in terms of the business world, from the oil and railroad industries to how the inner workings of businesses and corporations should be run in order to ensure ultimate success and wealth. And finally, he truly set the course for what it means to be a successful philanthropist. While the eradication of hookworm in the Southern regions would alone have merited him becoming one of the 20th century's greatest humanitarians, it was unfortunately his damaged reputation that would secure the fact that he would never receive due credit for his philanthropic endeavors that would go on to change so many lives in the United States.

Chapter Seven:

The Conclusion

From the earliest years of his life, John Davison Rockefeller was a man who strived to accomplish everything that he set in motion to achieve. He was a man who was honest, humble, genuine, generous, and incredibly intelligent. From his earliest days as a young boy in New York to a young man striving to reach his goals to becoming a successful man who had obtained wealth and achievements beyond his wildest imaginations, he was an individual who we can most certainly all learn something from and about. John D. Rockefeller was a man who was destined for all-out greatness.

However, in terms of American history, John D. Rockefeller is also a polarizing figure in the way that he was not a man who was wholly pure nor was he wholly evil. And while he was astutely brilliant in terms of being capable of acquiring the wealth that he did, however, it was the mannerisms in which he went about attaining that wealth that truly make one question the whole-hearted good nature of Rockefeller. He was ambitious, yes, however, he was also ruthless, and more often than not, conniving with regards to the tactics that he used to bring down corporations, both large and small, for his own ultimate gain. One important thing that we can learn from Rockefeller is the fact that ambition can drive one to each and every corner of the earth simply to be able to acquire both wealth and fortune. We kno

this because Rockefeller, by way of sheer ambition a

determination, would go on to become the wealthiest man

American history.

Rockefeller decimated his foes in the oil industry, tl

railroad industry, and any business who stood in his path

greatness. His company, the Standard Oil Company, was one th

was so incredibly powerful and abundant that the Supreme Cou

had to intervene by way of developing and implementing tl

Anti-Trust Act of 1890 to split the company up in what wou

prove to be a futile attempt at controlling it.

Rockefeller once stated that he was inclined to s

opportunities in every disaster. And that is precisely how he ro

to achieve such greatness. He took advantage of uniq

opportunities where others likely failed. Never once did l

complain about economic upheaval, and quitting was not a wo

in his vocabulary. He instead opted to observe the events th

were happening around him as they unfolded. He saw panic as

learning opportunity, and it was this intense methodology of se

discipline that granted Rockefeller the opportunity to be able

seize the advantage over countless obstacles that occurr

throughout his life.

He saw disasters rationally, never panicked, and nev

made rash decisions. Rockefeller saw benefits with regards

each and every disaster, and he transformed his mindset from taking a negative situation and turning it into a learning experience that he would develop into a skill set, and that led him to creating wealth beyond all expectations. Whether you view Rockefeller in a "survival of the fittest" Darwinian sense or even as more of an Alexander the Great type figure who was simply seeking to create his own empire, what we can really learn from John D. Rockefeller is that you do not survive in the corporate world simply on human feeling and emotion. You either become the player or the pawn in this game of life. And Rockefeller was most certainly the strategic player who ultimately won the game.

John Davison Rockefeller had worked his entire life to achieve great success. When he was 86 years old, he wrote this poem. Whether you choose to love him or loathe him, it sheds a more light on the genuine man himself.

"I was early taught to work, as well as play.
My life has been one long happy holiday,
Full of work and full of play.
I dropped the worry on the way,
And God was good to me every day."

9 7 9 8 5 6 6 0 2 2 6 0 4